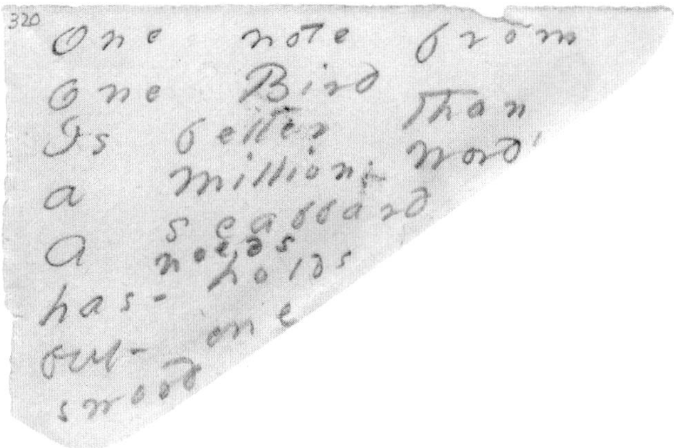

One note from
One Bird
Is better than
a million words

A scabbard
has-
holds
out-
one

notes

swords

Emily Dickinson
The Gorgeous Nothings

Marta Werner

Jen Bervin

with a Preface by Susan Howe

CHRISTINE BURGIN / NEW DIRECTIONS
in association with Granary Books

An image of the poem "Eternity will be": by permission of The Houghton Library,
Harvard University, MS Am 1118.5 (B3) © The President and Fellows of Harvard College
Images of all other facsimiles by permission of the Frost Library, Amherst College, © Amherst College

A Christine Burgin/New Directions Book published in association with Granary Books.

A limited edition of *The Gorgeous Nothings* was originally published as an artist's book by Steve Clay of Granary Books.

Grateful acknowledgment is made to Steve Clay of Granary Books; to Leslie Morris, Curator of Modern Books
and Manuscripts of The Houghton Library of the Harvard College Library; to Michael Kelly, Head of Archives &
Special Collections, Frost Library, Amherst College; and to Margaret Dakin, Archives & Special Collections
Specialist, Frost Library, Amherst College. For complete acknowledgments please see page 253.

Manufactured in China. Christine Burgin/New Directions Books are printed on acid-free paper.
First published as a Christine Burgin/New Directions Book in 2013.

Design and composition by Laura Lindgren.

Library of Congress Cataloging-in-Publication Data

Dickinson, Emily, 1830–1886.
  [Poems. Selections]
  The Gorgeous Nothings / Emily Dickinson, Marta L. Werner, Jen Bervin ;
with a preface by Susan Howe.
    pages cm
  Includes index.
  ISBN 978-0-8112-2175-7 (acid-free paper)
  1. Dickinson, Emily, 1830–1886—Manuscripts. 2. Dickinson, Emily, 1830–1886—
Criticism and interpretation. 3. Artists' books—Specimens. 4. Manuscripts,
American—Facsimiles. I. Werner, Marta L., 1964– II. Bervin, Jen. III. Title.
  PS1541.A6 2013
  811'.4—dc23
                                            2013016459

New Directions Books are published for James Laughlin by
New Directions Publishing Corporation
80 Eighth Avenue, New York, NY 10011

Christine Burgin books are published by
The Christine Burgin Gallery
239 West 18th Street, New York, NY 10011

1 3 5 7 9 10 8 6 4 2

Contents

Preface

Susan Howe

Wallace Stevens famously says that "Poetry is the scholar's art." In *The Gorgeous Nothings* a textual scholar and a visual artist have combined to create an exhibit in book form: the facsimile reproductions with transcriptions of the envelope writings of Emily Dickinson.

I grew up on the Thomas H. Johnson edition of *The Collected Poems* published in 1951. That is how I first knew and loved this poet of poets. I believed I was reading exactly what she had written—I found the dashes and capitals both radical and formal. The measure equally so until, in 1981, Ralph Franklin's facsimile edition of the *Manuscript Books* showed the same words, but with increasingly different line breaks, spread across the entire space of a page. Many poems contained variant word lists as part of the texts themselves. They were grouped together in various packets. There was now a possibility that these groupings might have been intended as serial works. But Franklin didn't provide transcriptions. Perhaps this is the reason it has taken such a long time for scholars of her work to look at what his labor brought to light. Franklin's updated variorium edition of *The Collected Poems*, with chronological and other changes, continued to ignore the visual and acoustic aspects of the manuscripts that are particularly obvious in the late fragments and drafts. For almost twenty years few poets and fewer scholars, after seeing the originals, have dared to show us the ways in which what we thought we saw was not really what was there. Thankfully, the Amherst College Library has recently made digitalized images of the manuscripts in their possession available to readers online. Yet it has always been my dream to see some of these late manuscripts in a book, with transcriptions, so the reader can look, and touch, and turn from one to another. I also wish that someday they will exhibited in a gallery situation because so often these singular objects balance between poetry and visual art. I am thrilled that Marta Werner, who has been working on the late fragments and drafts for two decades, has collaborated with the visual artist Jen Bervin to produce this marvelous edition.

For Proust, a fragment is a morsel of time in its pure state; it hovers between a present that is immediate and a past that once had been present. Can a mark on paper surprise itself at the instant of writing? Dickinson's later work often demonstrates that it can embrace contingency while capturing a moment *before*. Points of contact by ear, touch, and sight. Perhaps she conceived of a sentence or line as law-bound in the relation of simple elementary components, yet open, unbounded, and contingent. Viewing these "envelopes" as visual objects, while at the same time reading her words for sound and sense, one needs to seize upon luck and accidents—slips on paper slips.

Does form envelop everything? Can a thought hear itself see? These writings are suggestive, not static. How do you grasp force in its movement in a printed text? Is there any correct way to clear this entangled primal paper forest? Is there an unwritable unknown poem that exceeds anything the technique of writing can do? We will never know. Maybe this is her triumph. She has taken her secret to the grave and will not give up the ghost.

To arrive as if by telepathic electricity and connect without connectives. On the 14th of May, 1882, she wrote to Judge Otis P. Lord after hearing of his sudden illness: "Would I write a telegram? I asked the Wires how you did, and I attached my name."

In the case of mere paper envelopes, indifferent to risk and reverse, she has broken the epistolary seal. It has taken years and years for this aspect of Emily Dickinson to be made visible. When she was only sixteen she wrote, in a letter to her friend Abiah Root, "Let us strive together to part with time more reluctantly, to watch the pinions of the fleeting moment until they are dim in the distance & the new coming moment claims our attention." *The Gorgeous Nothings* claims our attention with a new Emily Dickinson. This edition itself is a work of art.

Studies in Scale

An Introduction by Jen Bervin

The Gorgeous Nothings is an excerpt from Emily Dickinson's manuscript A 821.
In choosing it as the title for this project, I was thinking of Dickinson's own
definition for *nothing* in a letter: "By homely | gifts and | hindered Words the
human | heart is told of nothing – 'Nothing' is | the force that renovates | the
World –"[1] and her definition for *no*: "the wildest | word we consign | to Language."[2]
These "gorgeous nothings" are *that* kind of nothing.

These manuscripts are sometimes still referred to as "scraps" within Dickinson
scholarship. Rather, one might think of them as the sort of "small fabric" Dickinson
writes of in one corner of the large envelope interior, A 636 / 636a: "Excuse |
Emily and | her Atoms | The North | Star is | of small | fabric but it | implies | much |
presides | yet."[3] The writing is small in relation to the compositional space, floating in
its firmament. This poem exemplifies Dickinson's relationship to scale so perfectly.
When we say *small*, we often mean less. When Dickinson says *small*, she means fabric,
Atoms, the North Star.

The concept of the "atom" emerges in ancient Greek philosophy as the idea of
"the smallest hypothetical body." At the outset of the nineteenth century, modern
atomic theory recasts the atom in chemical terms.[4] In 1830 Emily Dickinson is
born in Amherst, Massachusetts. She is thirty-five years old when the Civil War
ends and Johann Josef Loschmidt first measures the size of a molecule of air. In
the range of philosophic, scientific, and popular definitions for *atom* in the *OED*,
we also find a dust mote, the smallest medieval measure of time, "the twinkling of
an eye," and this apt, obsolete meaning too: "At home."[5]

This enigmatic poet who signs letters "Jumbo" or "Your Rascal" or "Your
Scholar" is petite by physical standards, but vast by all others. "My little Force
explodes –"[6] she writes to her future editor Thomas Wentworth Higginson in
1862, during a stretch when she is writing on average three hundred poems a
year. Emily Dickinson, one of the greatest American poets, wrote approximately
1,800 distinct poems within 2,357 poem drafts and at least 1,150 letters and prose
fragments—a total of 3,507 pieces before her death at the age of fifty-five.[7] On the

triangular flap of the envelope seal A 252, we find this fleeting message inscribed in lines winnowing down to a single word at the tip: "In this short Life | that only [merely] lasts an hour | How much – how | little – is | within our | power."

Dickinson's writing materials might best be described as epistolary. Everything she wrote—poems, letters, and drafts, in fascicles, on folios, individual sheets, envelopes, and fragments—was predominantly composed on plain, machine-made stationery.[8] "Preserve the backs of old letters to write upon," wrote Lydia Maria Child in *The Frugal Housewife*, a book Dickinson's father obtained for her mother when Emily was born. It opens: "The true economy of housekeeping is simply the art of gathering up all the fragments, so that nothing is lost. I mean fragments of *time* as well as *materials*."[9] Dickinson's envelope writings convey a sense of New England thrift and her relationship to the larger household economy of paper, but they also disclose private spaces within that household: the line "we should respect | the seals of | others –" inscribed next to the gummed seal of A 842 resounds.

Dickinson's poems and correspondence attest to the considerable care she gave to the ritual act of opening a letter. These envelopes have been opened well beyond the point needed to merely extract a letter; they have been torn, cut, and opened out completely flat, rendered into new shapes. To understand how forcefully Dickinson is manipulating the form of the page itself, take a simple household envelope and see how many of these forms you can re-create. You will quickly find that what looks simple, simply is not. There is not one instance here of an envelope reopened out into its die-cut shape. Look with care: what may look like a whole envelope is only one face of it, slit open. Where do those cuts fall and what shape do they prefigure when the space is opened out? How are some cut edges so surgically clean? At Amherst College Library, Margaret Dakin has acquired what is believed to be Emily Dickinson's lap desk; its painted wooden surface is positively riddled with myriad fine cuts. Though the written compositions may show considerable speed of thought and hand, Dickinson was not blindly grabbing scraps in a rush of inspiration, as is most often supposed, but rather reaching for writing surfaces that were most likely collected and cut in advance, prepared for the velocity of mind.

When Dickinson approached her compositional space to write, she was reading and responding to her materials, angling the page to write in concert with the light rule and laid lines in the paper, using internal surface divisions, such as overlapping planes of paper, to compose in a number of directional fields. Sometimes Dickinson's writing fills the space of the envelope like water in a vessel or funnels into the triangular shape of the flap. Often she invents columns, typically two, to further divide the space, demonstrating a propensity to break poem lines shorter and shorter. She draws additional line segments or arcs to further divide the compositional space. One would think that such a space would feel carved up, crammed, but it doesn't. The page feels bigger yet, as if there has been an *insertion* of space.[10]

"These manuscripts should be understood as visual productions," writes Susan Howe in *The Birth-mark.*[11]

In assembling *The Gorgeous Nothings* we were guided by this directive and specifically selected work that foregrounds Dickinson's experiments with visual form and variants on the page. We have favored this understanding in our presentation of manuscript facsimiles; each is reproduced actual size, front and back, accompanied by a transcription. This gathering of manuscripts presents all the works composed on envelopes or postal wrappers that Marta Werner has been able to trace to date. The envelope writings are not a series or discrete body of works. Each envelope has its own complex constellation of affiliations with manuscript drafts one can trace through sources in the Directory (page 243). These envelopes, spanning the years 1864 through 1886, are culled from 1,414 contemporaneous poem drafts and 887 letter drafts.[12]

We often gauge a writer's intentions by her published work, or by work she submitted for publication during her lifetime, but Dickinson offers no such certainties. Dickinson rejected print publication of her poems. In a letter to Higginson, she explains: "I smile when you suggest that I delay 'to publish' – that being foreign to my thought as Firmament to Fin. If fame belonged to me, I could not escape her – if she did not, the longest day would pass me on the chase – and the approbation of my Dog would forsake me – then – My Barefoot Rank is better–."[13] Yet she was not secretive about the fact that she was writing poems;

she sent more than three hundred poems to recipients in letters—letters that were often indistinguishable from poetry.

In *Black Riders: The Visible Language of Modernism*, Jerome McGann writes, "Dickinson's scripts cannot be read as if they were 'printer's copy' manuscripts, or as if they were composed with an eye toward some state beyond their handcrafted textual condition." He continues, "Emily Dickinson's poetry was not written *for* a print medium, even though it was written *in* an age of print. When we come to edit her work for bookish presentation, therefore, we must accommodate our typographical conventions to her work, not the other way around."[14] Throughout the late nineteenth and twentieth centuries, editors have painstakingly brought that work to the public for the most part "the other way around." Even in the most trusted scholarly editions, editors have restructured Dickinson's poems for print in opposition to the manuscripts, consistently overriding her line breaks, systematically deconstructing (or in reading editions, omitting) her formal construction of variant words and punctuation. Without manuscripts present, the reader cannot know how those editorial omissions and decisions have affected meaning.

Dickinson's manuscripts themselves, and the forms and experiments borne out in them, are the most authentic register of her intentions. Of the 3,507 poems, letters, drafts, and fragments Dickinson wrote, approximately a third of the manuscripts have been published in facsimile thus far.[15] The first substantial view of these appeared in 1981 in *The Manuscript Books of Emily Dickinson: A Facsimile Edition*, two volumes that include 1,147 poem facsimiles—the "fascicles," forty discrete packets of poems Dickinson assembled and tied with a stitch, as well as unbound sets. In 1996 Marta Werner published a new array of strikingly different visionary late works—forty manuscripts in *Emily Dickinson's Open Folios: Scenes of Reading, Surfaces of Writing*—followed in 2007 by *Radical Scatters: Emily Dickinson's Late Fragments and Related Texts, 1870–1886*, an extensive digital archive bringing forth one hundred and thirty-two more manuscripts. Werner's pioneering diplomatic transcriptions were the first to accurately reflect Dickinson's manuscripts typographically in book form.

To represent a Dickinson poem accurately in print, to "accommodate our typographic conventions to her work," is quite a demanding task. Dickinson's manipulation of textual space is elastic in the manuscripts: her sprawling headlong letterforms, ambiguous capitalization, gestural punctuation, scale shifts in variant words, extremely short lines, and expansive spatial placement of words on the page trouble even a visually minded transcription. These new transcriptions were created with the aim of a clean, legible text to act as *a key into*—not *a replacement for*—the manuscripts. If our interpretation of Dickinson's script errs, each manuscript is present to make its own determinations and ambiguities known.[16]

Dickinson's early manuscripts are predominantly written in ink; from 1864 to 1865 they are mostly in pencil, and thereafter both pen and pencil are used until the year 1878, when "the pen is almost entirely discarded."[17] All of the envelope poems are written in pencil. Unlike a fountain pen, a pencil stub, especially a very small one, fits neatly, at the ready, in the pocket of a dress. In an early letter to her brother, Austin, she wrote "This is truly extempore, Austin—I have no notes in my pocket,"[18] suggesting that there were typically jottings accumulating there. Dickinson's one surviving dress has a large external pocket on the right side, where her hand would fall easily at rest. The economy of the pocket is worth considering. An envelope is a pocket. An envelope refolds discreetly, privately, even after it has been sliced completely open. Emily Dickinson sent this minuscule two-inch-long pencil (pictured below) in a letter to the Bowles, "If it had no pencil, | Would it try mine – "[19] wryly nudging them to write. It was enveloped in a letter folded into thirds horizontally, pinned closed at each side.

Notes

1. *The Letters of Emily Dickinson*, 3 vols., edited by Thomas H. Johnson, with Theodora Ward (Cambridge, MA: The Belknap Press of Harvard University Press, 1958), L1563.

2. See Amherst College manuscript A 739: "Dont you know you | are happiest while | I withhold and | not confer – dont | you know that | 'No' is the wildest | word we consign | to Language? | You do, for you | know all things –" Amherst College Digital Collections, Emily Dickinson Collection, https://acdc.amherst.edu.

3. Manuscript H B 103 at Houghton Library, a letter written in pencil, folded horizontally in thirds, from Emily Dickinson to Susan Gilbert Dickinson from the early 1880s, carries another version of this text: "Excuse Emily | and her Atoms – | The 'North | Star' is of | small fabric, | but it denotes | much –" *Letters*, L774.

4. Dickinson would have been familiar with scientific developments through Mount Holyoke Academy and was an avid reader of newspapers, periodicals, and literature. For more on this, see Jack L. Capps's *Emily Dickinson's Reading, 1836–1886* (Cambridge, MA: Harvard University Press, 1966). A number of writers Dickinson read are using the word, most notably George Eliot and Ralph Waldo Emerson. Dickinson uses the word *atom* differently in eleven poems: P376, P410, P515, P600, P664, P889, P954, P1178, P1191, P1231, and P1239 (A 339, "Risk is the Hair | that holds the Tun"), *Poems* 1955.

5. *The Oxford English Dictionary*, 2nd ed. (Oxford: Oxford University Press, 1989).

6. *Letters*, L271.

7. The count is based on the total number of poem drafts indicated in *Poems* 1998. The tally of letters and prose fragments is from *Letters*. It's quite likely the number of actual letters was higher, diminished by the nineteenth-century custom of burning correspondence.

8. See Ralph Franklin's *The Editing of Emily Dickinson: A Reconsideration* (Madison, WI: University of Wisconsin Press, 1967), and *The Manuscript Books of Emily Dickinson* (Cambridge, MA: Belknap Press of Harvard University Press, 1981).

9. Jay Leyda, ed., *The Years and Hours of Emily Dickinson*, vol. 1 (New Haven, CT: Yale University Press, 1960), 16. Lydia Maria Child, *The Frugal Housewife*, 2nd ed. (Boston, MA: Carter & Hendee, 1830).

10. The tendency in Dickinson's late manuscripts is toward larger spaces between letters and words, short, heavily enjambed lines that amplify space, and smaller, yet more frequent punctuation marks. For more on this, see *The Dickinson Composites* (New York: Granary Books, 2010).

11. Susan Howe, "These Flames and Generosities of the Heart: Emily Dickinson and the Illogic of Sumptuary Values," *The Birth-mark: Unsettling the Wilderness in American History* (Middletown, CT: Wesleyan University Press, 1993), 141.

12. *Letters*, *Poems* 1998.

13. *Letters*, L265.

14. Jerome McGann, *Black Riders: The Visible Language of Modernism* (Princeton, NJ: Princeton University Press, 1993), 38.

15. See also Polly Longsworth, ed., *The Master Letters of Emily Dickinson* (Amherst, MA: Amherst College Press, 1986), and *Emily Dickinson: A Letter* (Amherst, MA: Oliphant Press, Friends of the Amherst College Library, 1992).

16. The transcription offers readers a typographic "map" to consult while reading the manuscript facsimile. Century Gothic's rounded, fixed-width, sans-serif letterforms are intended as a translation (not an imitation) of her scripts. Dickinson's upper- and lower-case letterforms, punctuation, and markings are expressive and open to multiple readings. The typographic interpretation reflects our scholarly engagement with her scribal practice but in no way claims definitiveness, given such ambiguities. The size of the transcriptions—50 percent relative to the envelopes—reflects our belief that Dickinson's manuscript is the primary space to read her work and is the highest authority on all questions. Though it is finally impossible to represent all the spatial dynamics of Dickinson's handwritten documents, attempts were made (using InDesign) to reflect them through placement, kerning, leading, spacing, and type size within the line drawing of the envelope. Ultimately, it was our hope to keep the transcriptions as legible as possible and gesture back toward the "bright Orthography" of Dickinson's manuscripts.

17. See Theodora Ward's "Characteristics of the Handwriting," in *Poems* 1955. See also Theodora Ward's "Study of the Handwriting" in *Emily Dickinson's Letters to Dr. and Mrs. Josiah Gilbert Holland* (Cambridge, MA: Belknap Press of Harvard University Press, 1951).

18. *Letters*, L165.

19. *Poems* 1955, P921; *Poems* 1998, P184. The two pins pictured on the front of the Visual Index (p. 225) originally pinned this letter with the pencil closed. This manuscript can be viewed online at https://acdc.amherst.edu/view/asc:5717.

The Envelope Writings

A 105

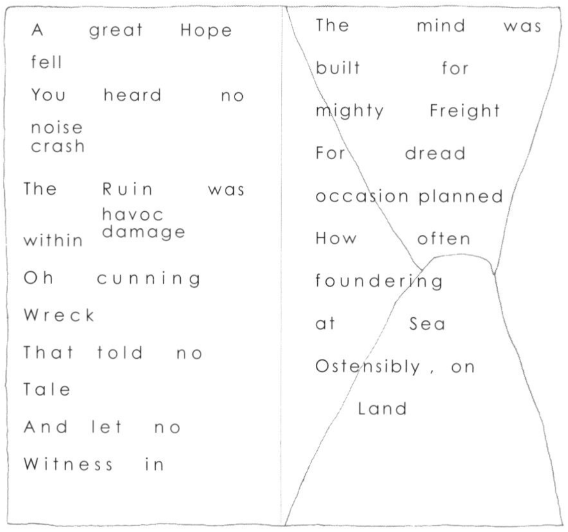

A great Hope
fell
You heard no
noise
crash
The Ruin was
havoc
within damage
Oh cunning
Wreck
That told no
Tale
And let no
Witness in

The mind was
built for
mighty Freight
For dread
occasion planned
How often
foundering
at Sea
Ostensibly , on
Land

A great hope
fell
You heard no
noise
  Crash
The Ruin was
within
  house Damage
Oh Cunning
wreck
that told no
tale
And let no
Witness in

the Mind was
built for
mighty Freight
for dread
occasion planned
how often
foundering
at Sea
Ostensibly, on
Land

A not admitting
of the wound
until it grows so
wide
that all my
Life had entered it
And ~~thoughts~~ there
were brought
beside -
   was space
      room

A Closing of the
simple Lid that
    Gate
opened to the sun
Until the hinder
Carpenter
      sovereign
Perpetual nail
it down -

A 105a

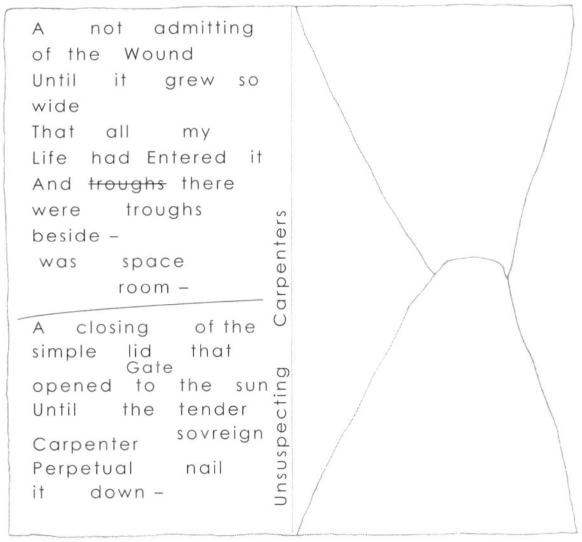

A   not   admitting
of the Wound
Until   it   grew so
wide
That   all   my
Life had Entered it
And ~~troughs~~ there
were   troughs
beside –
was   space
room –

A   closing   of the
simple   lid   that
        Gate
opened   to   the sun
Until   the   tender
              sovreign
Carpenter
Perpetual   nail
it   down –

Unsuspecting Carpenters

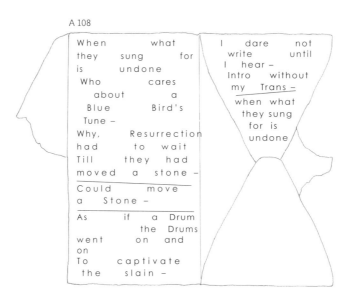

A 108

When   what
they   sung   for
is   undone
  Who   cares
    about   a
    Blue   Bird's
    Tune –
Why,   Resurrection
had   to   wait
Till   they   had
moved   a   stone –

Could   move
a   Stone –

As   if   a   Drum
          the   Drums
went   on   and
on
To   captivate
    the   slain –

I   dare   not
    write   until
I   hear –
Intro   without
my   Trans –
when   what
they   sung
for   is
undone

When what
they sung for
is undone
Who cares
about a
Blue Bird's
tune -
Why, Resurrection
had to wait
till they had
moved a stone -

Could move
a Stone -

As if a Drum
        the Drums
went on and
on
to captivate
the slain -

I dare not
write until
I hear -,
Intro without
my Trans -

When what
they sung
for is
undone

Louisa Norcross"
writing

Miss Emily E. Dickinson.
Amherst.
Mass.

Virma

A Pang is more
conspicuous in Spring

In contrast with the
those
things that sing,
Not Birds entirely - but
Minds - Minute Effulgen -
And Winds - - cies

When what they sung
for is undone
who cares about
a Blue Bird's tune -
Why, Resurrection
had to wait
till they had moved
a Stone -

A 109

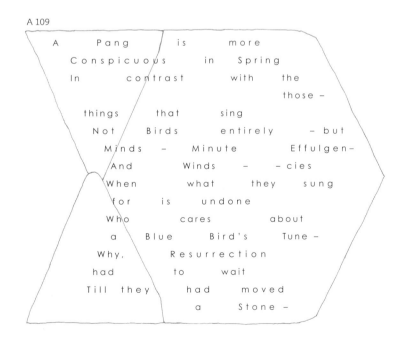

A   Pang   is   more
Conspicuous   in   Spring
In   contrast   with   the
     those –
things   that   sing
Not   Birds   entirely   – but
Minds –   Minute   Effulgen–
And   Winds –   –cies
When   what   they   sung
for   is   undone
Who   cares   about
a   Blue   Bird's   Tune –
Why,   Resurrection
had   to   wait
Till they   had   moved
a   Stone –

A 128

All   men   for   Honor
hardest   work
But   are   not   known
to   earn –
Paid   after   they   have
ceased   to   work
In   Infamy   or   Urn –

All men for honor
hardest work
But are not known
To earn —
Paid after they have
ceased to work
ased to work
In Infamy or Urn —

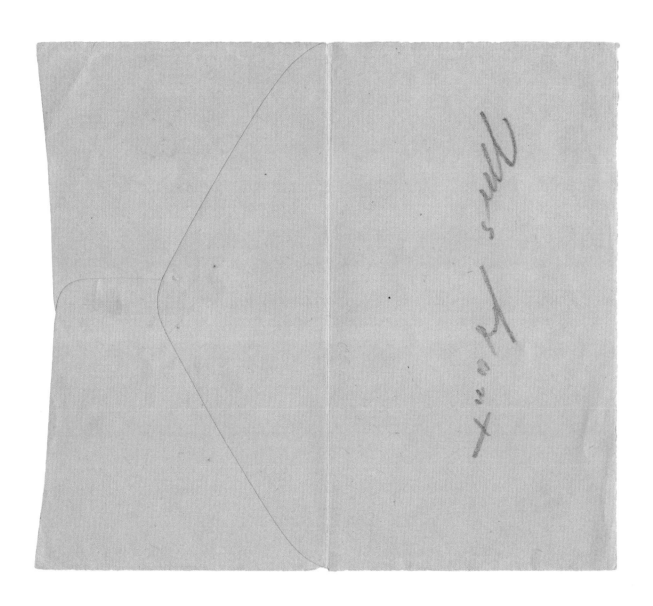

As old as Woe—
How old is that?
Some eighteen
thousand years—
As old as
Bliss
Joy—
How old is
that or
the age of that
they are of
equal years—

together
Chiefest—the
chiefs
are found

But—The seldom
side of side—
not from
neither of
them tho'
he her
can
may
human

nature
hide

A 139

As   old   as Woe –
How   old   is   that ?
Some   Eighteen
thousand   years –
As   old   as
Bliss
Joy –
How   old   is
that   or
The   age   of that
They   are   of
Equal   years –

Together
Chiefest   they
  Chiefly
    are   found

But   ⌊tho seldom
side   by   side –
not   From
neither   of
them tho'
he   try
can
may
  Human
Nature
hide

A 140

As   Sleigh Bells   More   distant in
  sound
seem   in   Summer   an   instant
Or   Bees,   at   Than   Dawn
Christmas   show –   in   Timbuctoo –
          foreign   on
so   fairy –   so
fictitious –
The   individuals
do
Repealed   from
Observation –
A Party that we
          whom
knew –

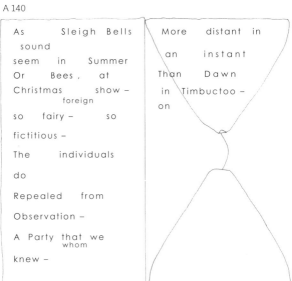

As Sleigh Bells
sound
seem in Summer
As Roses at-
Christmas show-
foreign
so faint, so
fictitious
the individuals
do.

Repealed from
Observation -
A Past that we
whom
knew.

more distant in
an instant
than than
in Tomorrow
in
on

Mrs Eliza M. Coleman.
Care Nd Lyman Coleman
Philadelphia.

Mrs
Helen Bertram
Harris

It will not harm
her magic back
that we, so far
obtain'd
Her distances
element
propitiate
As Branches
touch the wind

Not depend on
his notice far
east
But ready to
go on — Closer
further
simply
merely
'tis

'tis Glory's over-
tastelessness
that makes less
running pen our

We introduce
ourselves
to planets and
to flowers
But with
ourselves —
have Etiquettes
Embarrassments
And awes

A 145 / 146

It will not harm	We introduce
her magic pace	ourselves +
That we, so far	To Planets and
behind	to Flowers
Her distances	But with
Element	ourselves
propitiate	Have Etiquettes
As Branches	Embarrassments
touch the Wind	And awes

Not hoping for
his notice far
vast
But nearer to
Adore – closer
further
simply
merely
finer
'Tis Glory's over–
takelessness
That makes our
running poor

A 165

Death warrants are
supposed to ~~he~~
believed to be ~~me~~
An Enginery of
Equity
hazardous
A merciful mistake
A pencil in
dainty
an Idol's Hand

A Devotee has
oft consigned
To Crucifix
or Block
stake

cool - bland

Death warrants are
supposed to be
believed to be ~~will~~
an Engineer of
Equity, hazardous mistake
a merciful
a pencil in
        paint
an Idols Hard
a Devotee has
oft consigned
to crucifix
or Block
        stake

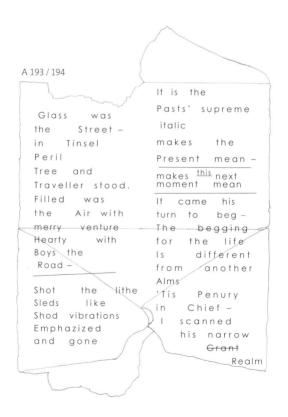

A 193 / 194

Glass was
the Street –
in Tinsel
Peril
Tree and
Traveller stood.
Filled was
the Air with
~~merry venture~~
Hearty with
Boys the
Road –

Shot the lithe
Sleds like
Shod vibrations
Emphazized
and gone

It is the
Pasts' supreme
italic
makes the
Present mean –
makes _this_ next
moment mean

It came his
turn to beg –
~~The begging~~
for the life
Is different
from another
Alms
'Tis Penury
in Chief –
I scanned
his narrow
~~Grant~~
Realm

Glass was
the Street —
in tinsel
Peril
Tree and
Traveller stood.
Filled was
the Air with
merry venture
Hearty with
Boys the
Road.

Shot the lithe
Sleds like
shod vibrations
Emphasized
and gone

It is the
Past's supreme
italic
makes the
Present mean —
makes this never
moment - mean

It came his
turn to beg —
the begging
for the life
Is different
from another
Alms
It is penury
his Child —
he scanned
his narrow
Realm

Western Union Telegrapn Co.

WILLIAM ORTON, Pres't.

Vinnie Dickinson
Care Judge Lord

No: ______

Charges. Paid

I gave him leave
to live
lest Gratitude
revive the snake
~~thought~~ me ~~[illegible]~~

though
Smuggled
my - his
Reprieve

[illegible]
~~[illegible]~~
~~[illegible]~~

I gave
him leave
to live so

Telegra

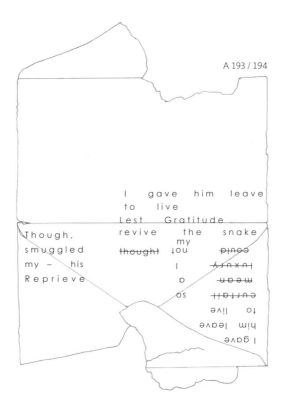

I   gave   him   leave
to   live
Lest   Gratitude
revive   the   snake
                my
Though,   thought   not   could
smuggled   I   luxury
my – his   mean
Reprieve   a   curtail
                so   to   live
                him   leave
                I gave

A 201

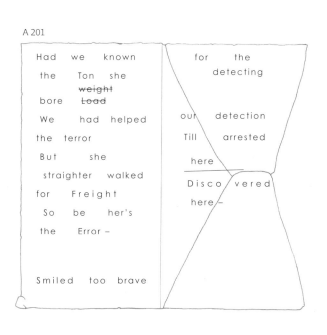

Had   we   known

the   Ton   she

bore   ~~weight~~

~~Load~~

We   had helped

the terror

But   she

straighter   walked

for   Freight

So   be   her's

the   Error –

Smiled   too brave

for   the

detecting

our   detection

Till   arrested

here

Disco vered

here –

201

Had we known
the Ton she
bore ~~weight~~
We had helped
the minor
But she
~~straightly~~ walked
for Fright—
So we deny
the Error—

Smiles too brave

for the
detecting

our detection
till arrested
here
————
Discovered
here.

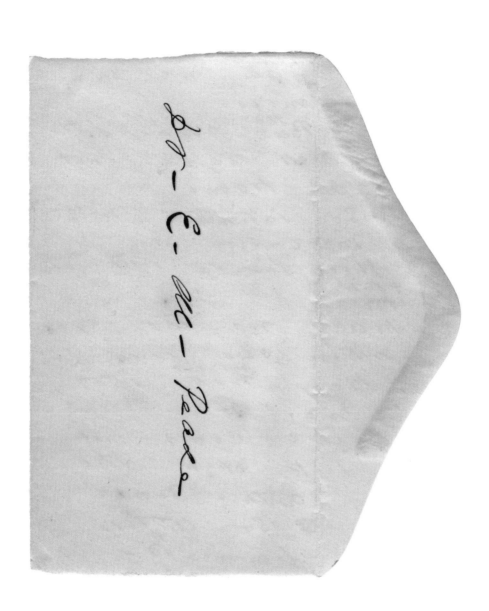

Dr. E. M. Peale

Had we our
senses
        tho'
But perhaps 'tis
well they're   not
at Home
So intimate with
Madness
He's liable with them
thers'
'tis
Had we the eyes
within our Head -
        prudent
How well that
we are Blind.
We could not
look opon The
Earth - Would
So utterly
unmoved -

A 202

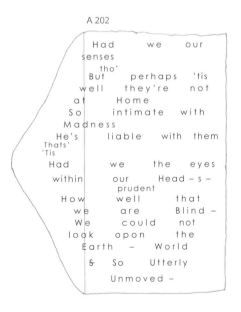

Had   we   our
senses
          tho'
But   perhaps   'tis
well   they're   not
at   Home
So   intimate   with
Madness
He's   liable   with them
Thats'
'Tis
Had   we   the   eyes
within   our   Head – s –
           prudent
How   well   that
        we   are   Blind –
We   could   not
look   opon   the
Earth   –   World

S   So   Utterly

Unmoved –

A 232

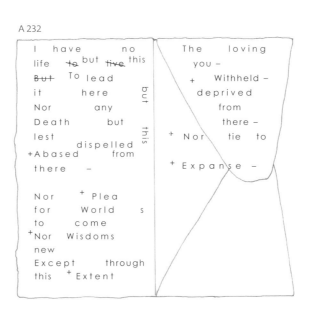

I have no
life but this –
To lead
it here –
Nor any
Death – but lest
dispelled –
+ Abased – from
there –

Nor Plea for
Worlds
to come –
+ Nor Wisdoms
new –
Except through
this + Extent

The loving
you –
+ Withheld –
deprived
from
there –
+ Nor tie to

+ Expanse –

I have no
life ~~to~~ out~~in~~ this   the loving
~~But~~ to lead   sou-
it here   + Withheld.
Nor any   deprived
death but   from
lest dispelled   there.
+ Abased from   + nor tie to
There -   + Expanse-

Nor +plea
for World s
to come
+Nor Wisdoms
new
Except through
This + Extent

A 236

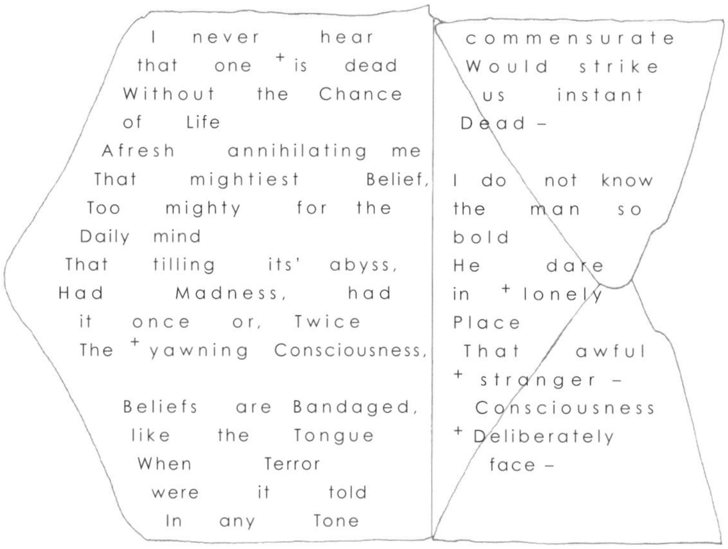

I never hear
that one + is dead
Without the Chance
of Life
Afresh annihilating me
That mightiest Belief,
Too mighty for the
Daily mind
That tilling its' abyss,
Had Madness, had
it once or, Twice
The + yawning Consciousness,

Beliefs are Bandaged,
like the Tongue
When Terror
were it told
In any Tone

commensurate
Would strike
us instant
Dead –

I do not know
the man so
bold
He dare
in + lonely
Place
That awful
+ stranger –
Consciousness
+ Deliberately
face –

I never hear
that one is dead
without the Chance
of Life

Afresh annihilating me
that mightiest Belief,
too mighty for the
Daily mind
that tilling it's abyss,
Had Madness, had
it - once or, twice
the + sarming Consciousness,

Beliefs are Bandaged,
like the tongue
when Terror
were it told
In any tone

Commensurate
would strike
us instant
Dead -

I do not know
the man so
bold
He dare
in lonely
Place,
that awful
+ stranger.
Consciousness
+ Deliberately
face -

+ that one has
died-
+ Consciousness
of this.
+ lonesome
- place- secret
place
+ look
+ squarely
in the face.

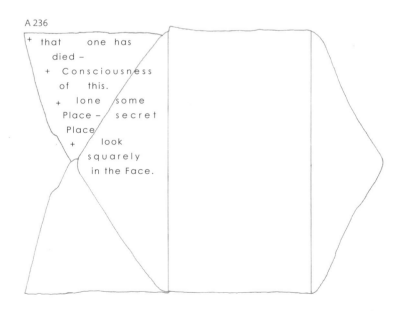

A 236

+ that　one has
　　died –
　　+ Consciousness
　　of　this.
　　+ lone some
　　Place – secret
　　Place
　　　+ look
　　　squarely
　　　in the Face.

A 252

In   this   short   Life
that   only   lasts an hour
        merely

    How   much —   how
    little — is
        within our
        power

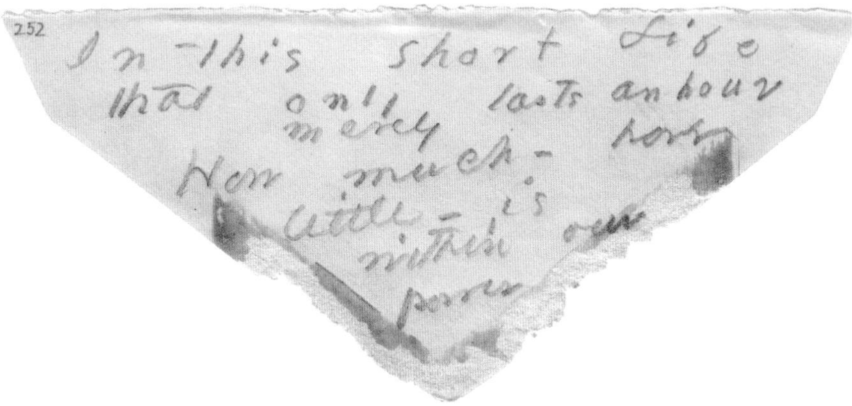

In this short life
that only lasts an hour
merely   how
How much - how
little - is
within our
power

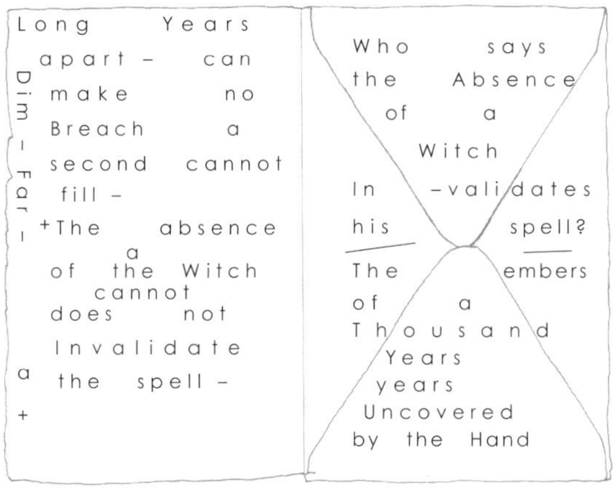

Long   Years
apart –   can
make   no
Breach   a
second   cannot
fill –
+The   absence
      a
of   the   Witch
      cannot
does   not
Invalidate
the   spell –

Dim – Far –

+

Who   says
the   Absence
of   a
        Witch
In   –validates
his   spell?
The   embers
of   a
Thousand
Years
years
Uncovered
by   the   Hand

Long Years
apart - can
make no
Breach a
second cannot
fill -

+ the absence
a Witch
of the Witch
does not cannot
Invalidate
a the spell -

+

Who says
the Absence
of a
Witch
In-validates
his spell?

the _____ embers

of a
Thousand
years
years
Uncovered
by the Hand

that
fondled
them
when
they
were
fire

gleam
and
understand

will

Miss Emma Dickinson

A 277

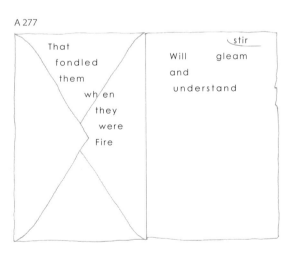

A 278

Look   back
on   Time
with   kindly
Eyes –
He   doubtless
did   his   best –
How   softly
sinks   that
                    his
trembling   Sun
In   Human
Nature's   West –

Look back
on time,
with kindly
Eyes—
He doubtless
did his best—
How softly
his
sinks that
trembling Sun
In Human
Nature's Nest—

myself compli-
ed were the
Pearls
What Legacy
could be

_____

Oh Magnanimity
My Visitor in
Paradise.

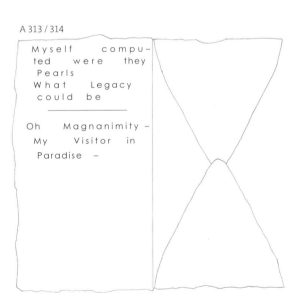

A 313 / 314

Myself   compu-
ted   were   they
Pearls
What   Legacy
could   be

Oh   Magnanimity —
My   Visitor   in
Paradise   —

A 316

Oh   Sumptuous

moment

Slower   go

~~Till   I~~   That   I
                Till
may   gloat   on
can
thee –
'Twill   never

be   the   same

to   starve

Now that I abundance
since
see –

Which   was   to

famish ,   then   or

now –

The   difference

of   Day
        to
Ask   him
unto   the   Gallows

led –   called

With   morning
By
in   the   Sky

76

On Scrupulous
moment —

Slower go
~~that~~ that I
Tide
may gloat on
can
~~[illegible]~~ .

I will never
be the same
to stairs
that I
Now abundance
since
see —

Which was it

famish, then
now.

the difference
of Day
10

Ask him
unto the Ballns
Ad — called
with morning
By
in the sky

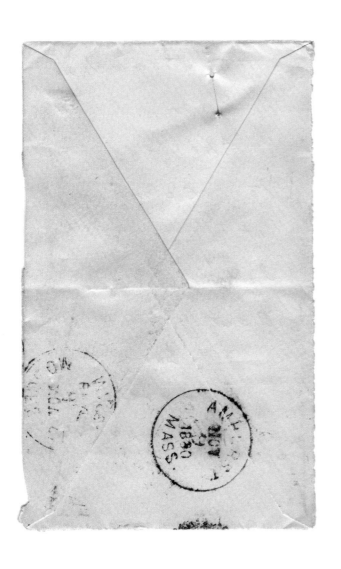

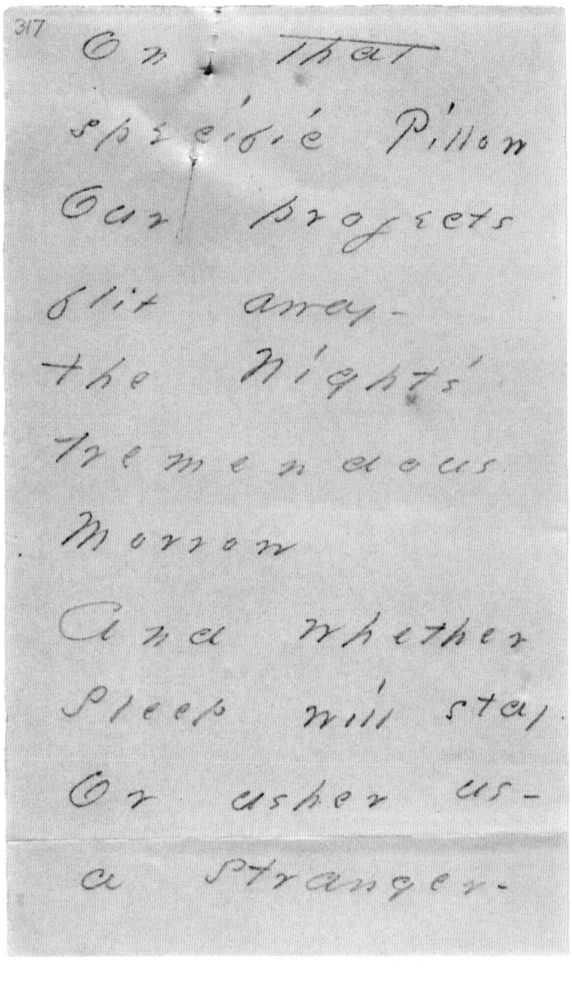

On that
specific Pillow
Our projects
flit away -
the Nights'
tremendous
Morrow

And whether
Sleep will stay,
Or usher us -
a Stranger -

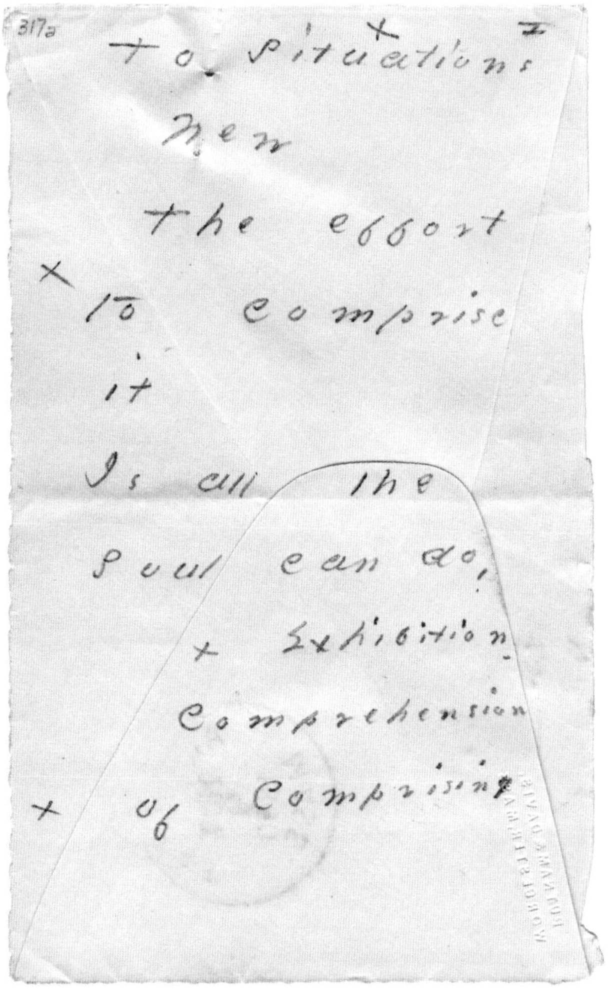

+ to, situations
new

the effort
× to comprise
it

Is all the
soul can do,
+ Exhibition
Comprehension
+ of Comprising

A 317

On   that
specific   Pillow
Our   projects
flit   away —
The   Nights'
Tremendous
Morrow
And   whether
Sleep   will stay
Or   usher   us —
a   Stranger —

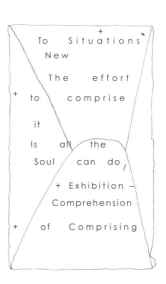

To   Situations
New
    The   effort
+   to   comprise
    it
Is   all   the
    Soul   can do
        + Exhibition —
    Comprehension
+   of   Comprising

A 320

One   note   from
One   Bird
Is   better   than
a   million words
A   scabbard
           needs
has – holds
but   one
sword

One   note   from
One   Bird
Is   better   than
a   Millions   words
a   scabbard
has - notes   holds
out-   one
sweet

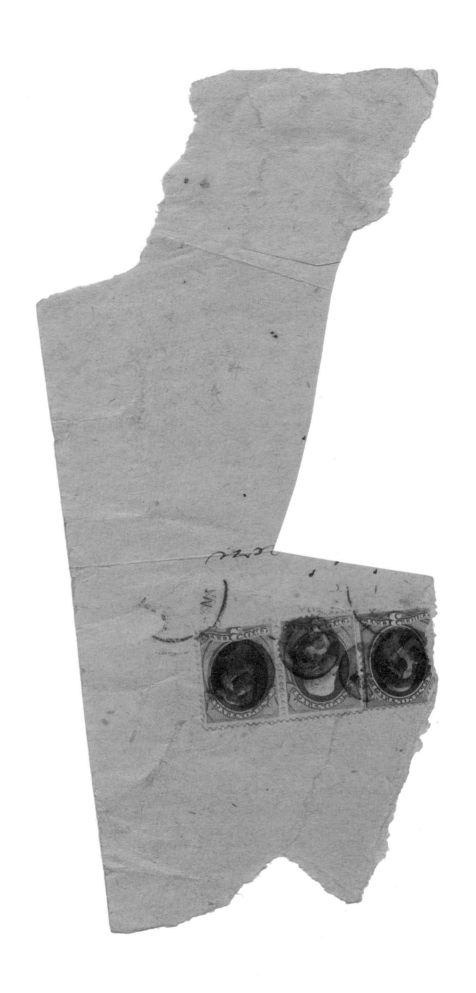

324

Our little
secrets
slink
away —
Beside
god; shall
not will
tell —
He kept
his word
a trillion
seers might me
And as well —
not as well
But for the
might only
delight
to make
each other
stare

Is there no
somet beneath
the sun
with this
that may
company

A 324

Our little
secrets
slink
away —
Beside
God's shall
not will
tell —
He kept
his word
a Trillion
years
And might we
not as well —
But for the
niggardly
delight
To make
each other
stare
Is there no
sweet beneath
the sun
With this
that may
compare —

A 332

Pompless
no   Life
can   pass
away –
The   lowliest   The   Hos –
career   pitable
To   the   Pall –
same pag –   A   this
eant wends   way
it's   way   beckons
as   that   spaciously
+ Exalted   there is
here –   world
How   cordial   a   Throne
is   the   for   all
Mystery   chair
                               seat
                               Each   oc
                               cupant   an
                                       Earl

332

Pompless - the Hos -
no Life quilialto
can pass away
the lowliest
career
to the
same Pag-
eant
it may
as
Established
per -
Nor
is
mislead

Pell -
a thir
may
[illegible]
[illegible]
their
[illegible]
for all
a hair
[illegible]
each of
cupant an
Earl

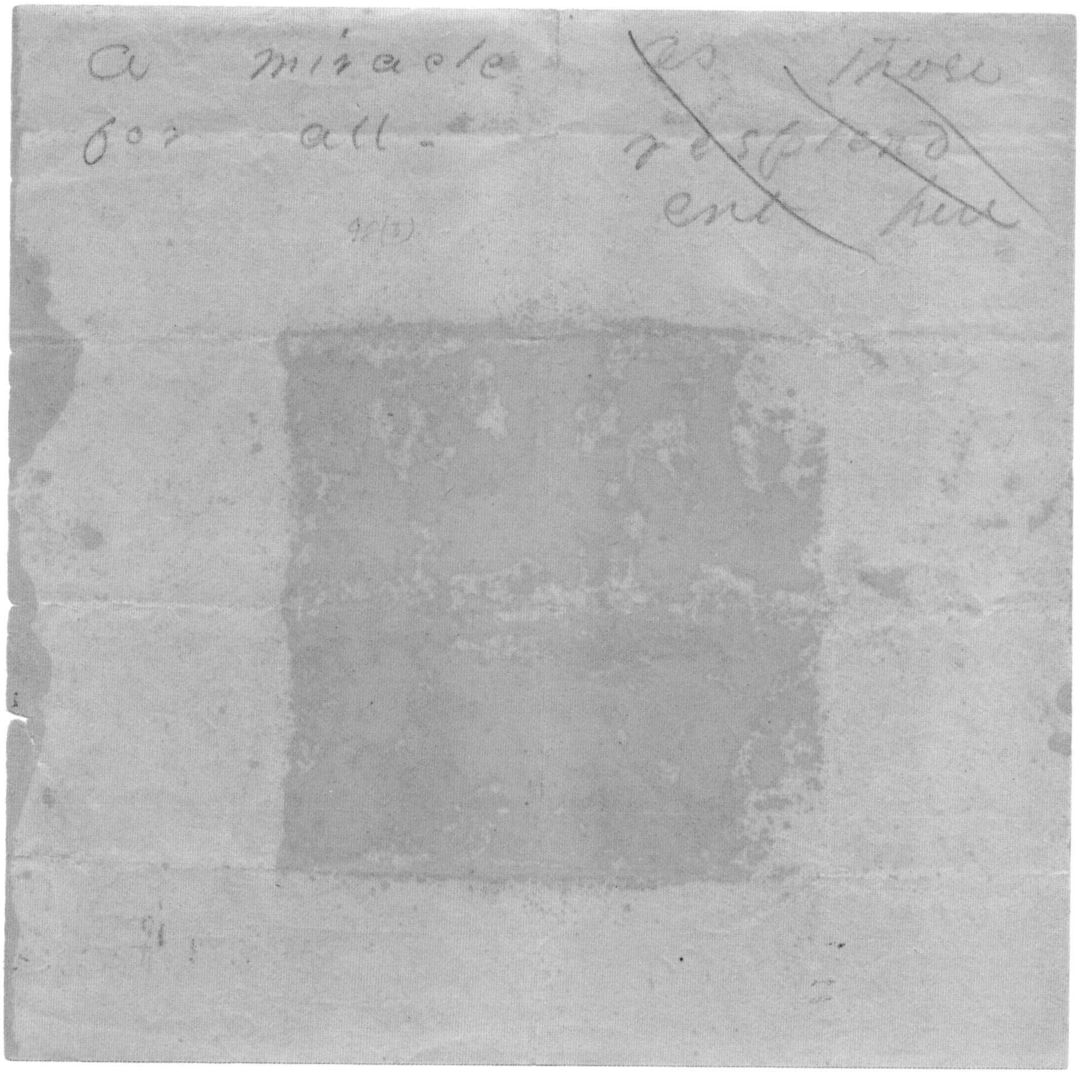

a miracle
for all.

es thou
resplend
ent hid

92(3)

A 332

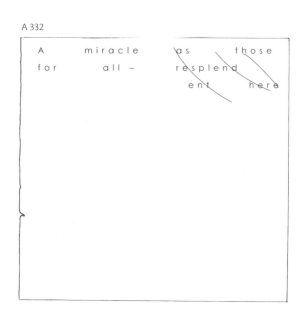

A   miracle   as   those
for   all —   resplend
ent   here

A 339

Risk is the Hair
that holds the Tun
Seductive in the Air –
That Tun is hollow –
but the Tun – one
With Hundred
+Weights – to spare –
Too ponderous to sus–
pect the snare
Espies that fickle
chair
And + seats itself
to be let go
By that perfidious
Hair –

The "foolish
Tun" the

Critics say –
While that
+ delusive
Hair + obliging –
Per – suasive
as Perdition,
Decoys
its' + Traveller
+Passenger

+ mounts
to be to
atoms hurled –
+ enchanting –

Risk [339] is the Hair
that holds the Tan
Seductive in the Air -
that tun is hollow -
but the tun - one
+ with Hundred
+ weights - to spare -
too ponderous to sus-
pect the snare
Espies that fickle
Chair
And seats itself
to be let go,
By that perfidious
Hair -

the "foolish
tun" the

Cities say -
While that
+ delusive
Hair + obliging.
Per- suasive
as Perdition,
+ ecstasy
+ it's Traveller
+ passenger

+ mounts
to be 1 to
alums hurled.
+ enchanting -

Dr. E. W. Pearce
Spring Grove
Illinois

107

A 351 / 352

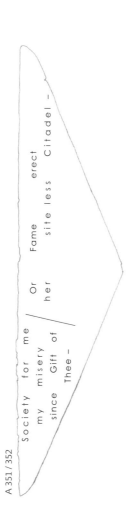

Society for me
my misery
since Gift of
Thee –

Or Fame erect
her site less Citadel –

A 355

Some   Wretched
creature ,   savior
take
Who   would Exult
to die
And   leave   for
thy   sweet
mercy's   sake
patience
Another   Hour
to   me
            human
My   Earthly
             Life
Hour to me

Same wretched
creature, savior
take

Who would revolt
to die
And leave our
thy sweet-
ness's sake
Patience
Another
to me
human
my earthly
Hour to me

Summer laid
her simple Hat
On it's boundless
Shelf.
Unobserved - a Ribbin
slipt   sanction
         fasten
Summon it - yourself.

Summer laid her supple Glove
In it's silvan Drawer -
Where   soberly   it - or as
        Where
    was she -
    the
    an   Abbais
                 Of Awe -
                (The
                 Demand
                 of Awe

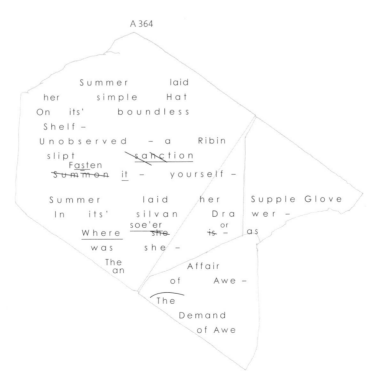

A 364

Summer   laid
her   simple   Hat
On   its'   boundless
Shelf —
Unobserved   —   a   Ribin
slipt   ~~sanction~~
    Fasten
~~Summon~~ it —   yourself —

Summer   laid   her   Supple Glove
In   its'   silvan   Dra wer —
         soe'er
Where   ~~she~~   ~~is~~ —   as
was   she —
            The
            an
                Affair
            of   Awe —
                The
                Demand
                of Awe

103

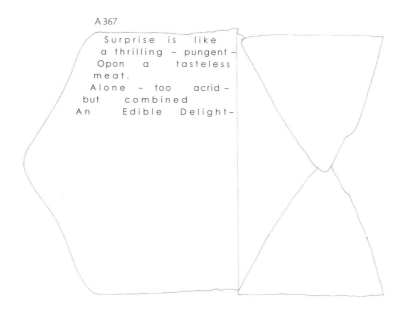

A 367

Surprise is like
a thrilling – pungent –
Opon a tasteless
meat.
Alone – too acrid –
but combined
An Edible Delight–

367 Surprise is like
   a thrilling - pungent -
Upon a tasteless
   meat.
Alone - too acrid -
   but - Combined
An Edible Delight.

Mr. E. W. Drake

Frank Girsert. for
Hotel Vendome.
Boston.
Mass.

She's brother there in Texas
Their father was a drunkard.

391

the Ditch
is dear to the
Drunken man
for is it not
his Bed - his
Advocate his
Edifice - The,
Hour safe his
fallen Head
his Disheveled
Sanctity -
Above him
is the Sky -
Oblivion bending
over him

A 391

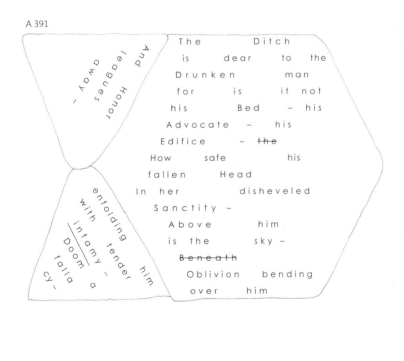

And Honor leagues away –

enfolding him
with   tender
infamy –
Doom   a
falla
cy –

The   Ditch
is   dear   to   the
Drunken   man
for   is   it   not
his   Bed   –   his
Advocate   –   his
Edifice   –   ~~the~~
How   safe   his
fallen   Head
In her   disheveled
Sanctity –
Above   him
is the   sky –
~~Beneath~~
Oblivion   bending
over   him

A 394 / 394a

The   fairest   Home   I   ever
knew
was   founded   in   an   Hour
By   Parties   also   that   I knew
A   spider   and   a   Flower –
A   manse   of   mechlin   and
of   Floss   –   Gloss   –   Sun –

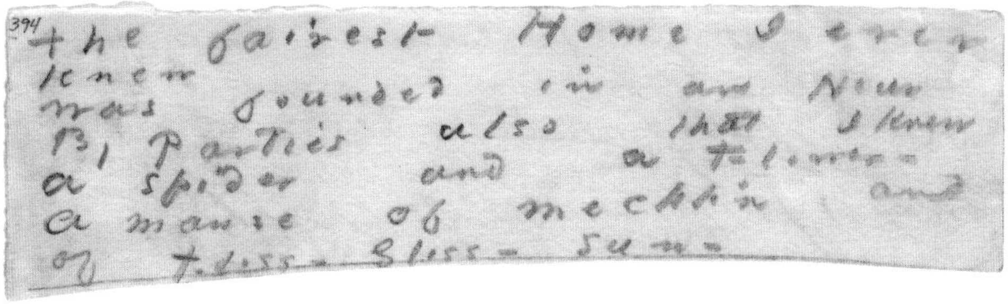

394

the fairest Home I ever
knew was founded in an Hour
By Parties also that I knew
a spider and a flower—
a manse of mechlin and
of Floss— Bliss— same

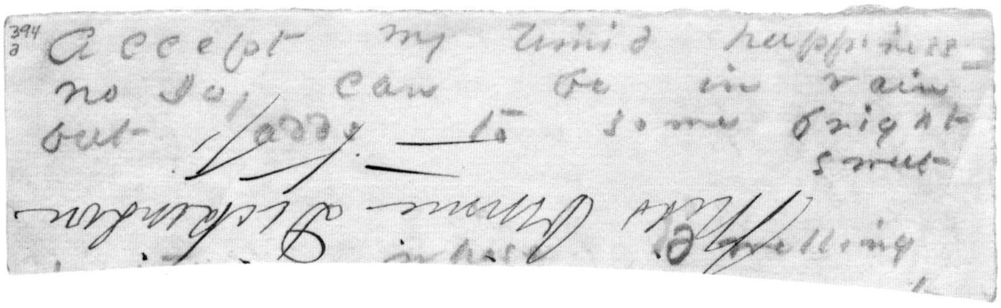

Accept my timid happiness—
no Joy can be in vain
but adds to some bright
sweet

A 394 / 394 a

Accept   my   timid happiness
no   Joy   can   be   in   vain
but   adds   to   some   bright
                                sweet
              whose   dwelling

A 416

The
Mushroom
is the Elf
of Plants –
At Evening
it is not –
At morning – in a Truffled
Hut
It stop upon a spot
As if it tarried always
And yet its' whole career
Is shorter than a
snake's delay
And fleeter
than a
+
Tare –

the
mushroom
is the Elf
of Plants.
At Evening
it is not -
At morning - in a Truffled
Hut
It stop opon a spot
As if it tarried always
And yet it's whole Career
Is shorter than a
snake's delay
And fleeter
than a
+
Tare -

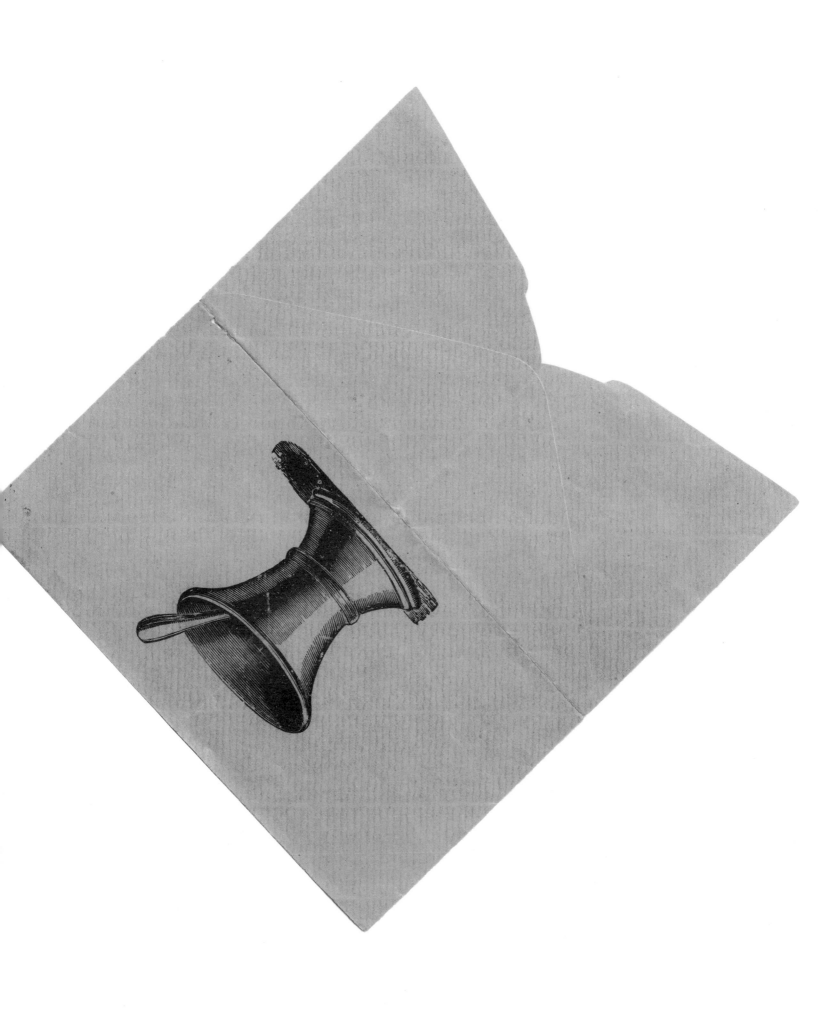

A 438

The   Spry Arms   The   Wind   could

of   the   Wind   wait   without the

If   I   could   Gate

crawl   between   Or   stroll   the

I have an Errand   Town   among –

imminent   Be   To   ascertain

To an adjoining   the   House

Zone –   if   soul's
                                And   is   the   soul
I   should   not   within
                                at   Home
care   to stop,
                                And   hold   the
My   Process   is
                                Wick   of   mine to
not   long
                                it

                                The long Arms

438

The spry Arms
of the Wind
If I could
crawl between
I have an errand
imminent
to an adjoining
Zone -
I should not
care to stop
My Process is
not long

the Wind could
wait without the
Gate
Or stroll the
Town among.
To ascertain
the House
And is the soul
within
at Home
And hold the
Wick of mine to

438a

to light, And
then relium—

Miss Emily Dickinson

A 438

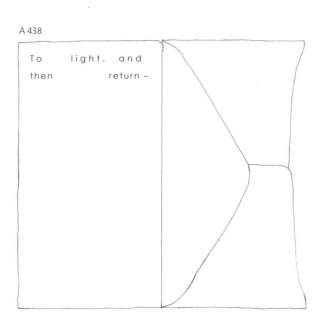

To   light,   and
then   return –

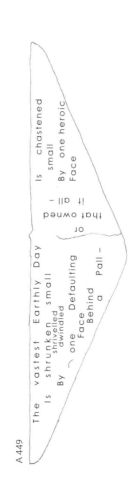

A 449

The vastest Earthly Day
Is shrunken small
shrivelled
dwindled
By ⁀ one Defaulting
Face
Behind a Pall –

Is chastened
small
By one heroic
Face

that owned it all –
or

Mrs Edward Dickinson
and Family

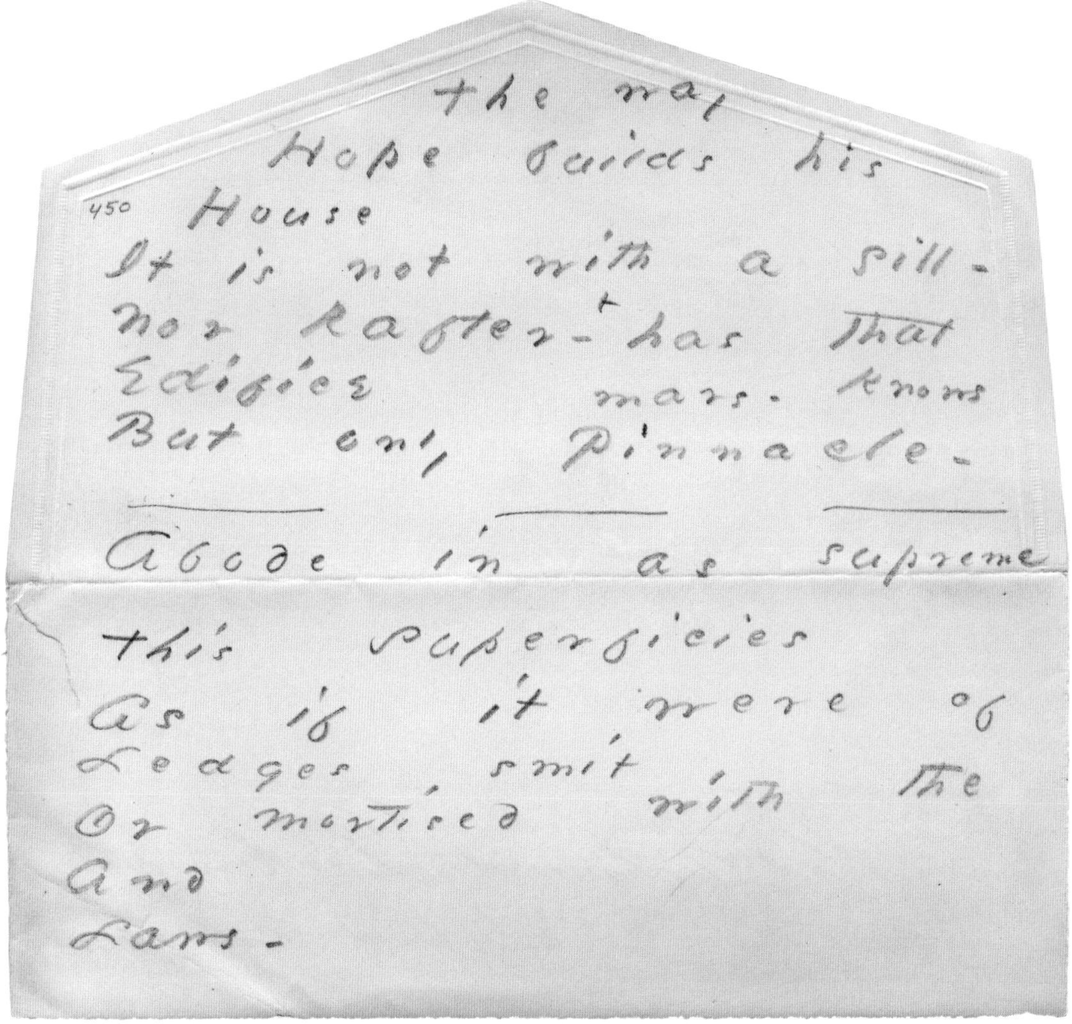

the rat
Hope builds his
House
It is not with a sill-
Nor Rafter-has that
Edifice
         mars. knows
But only Pinnacle-

_____ _____

Abode in   as   supreme

this Superficies
As if   it   were   of
Ledges , smit   the
Or mortised   with
And
Laws-

A 450

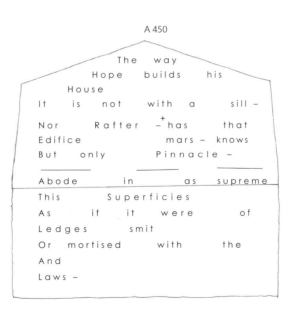

The way
Hope builds his
House
It is not with a sill –
Nor Rafter –⁺ has that
Edifice mars – knows
But only Pinnacle –

Abode in as supreme
This Superficies
As if it were of
Ledges smit
Or mortised with the
And
Laws –

A 463

was   never
Frigate li
like

that's
There's the
Battle of Burgoyne -
Over, every day,
By the Time
That Man and
Beast
Put their work
away -
"Sunset" sounds
majestic -
But that solemn
War
Could say
Comprehend it

You would
Chastened
stare -

A 464

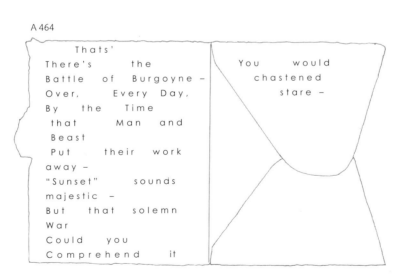

Thats'
There's   the
Battle   of   Burgoyne —
Over,   Every Day,
By   the   Time
that   Man   and
Beast
Put   their   work
away —
"Sunset"   sounds
majestic —
But   that   solemn
War
Could   you
Comprehend   it

You   would
chastened
stare —

A 479

Through   what
transports   of
Patience
I   reached   the
stolid   Bliss
To   breathe my
Blank   without
thee
Attest   me   this
and   this –
   By   that bleak
Exultation   .
I   won   as
   near as   this
Thy   privilege
of   dying
Abbreviate   me
this
Remit   me this
      and   this

Through what
transports of
Patience
I reached the
stolid Bliss
to breathe my
Blank without
thee

Attest me this
and this -
By that bleak
exultation
I won as
near as this -
thy privilege
of dying

Abbreviate me
this
Re-mit me this
and this

Miss Emily Dickinson,
Care Hon. Edward Dickinson,
Amherst,
Mass.

To   her
derided   Home
A   Weed   of
Summer   came –
She   did   not
know   her
station   low
Nor   ignominy's
Name –
Bestowed   a
Summer   long
Upon   a   fameless

Sustains him anywhere – her

[left column, inverted:]

Escutscheon –
the Buttercup's
a   Star –
Is   valid   as
lion's   Shield
the   Dande-
her   Bower –
As   Lady   from
from   Disdain
as   lightly
then   swept
Flower –

flower -

then swept
as lightly,
from Disdain
As had from
her Bower -
the Dande-
lion's Shield
Is valid as
a Star -
the Buttercup's
Escutcheon -

Sustains him in
amandere-
She did not know
her Station -
Summer came -
To her

o her
overflow Home
Summer came -
She did not beckon -
Went back -
You did not
Ignominiously -
Bestowed a
Name -
Summer long
Upon a Nameless

Leontodon's
Escutcheon
Sustains him
Anywhere.

A 488

Leontodon's

Escutcheon

Sustains him

anywhere –

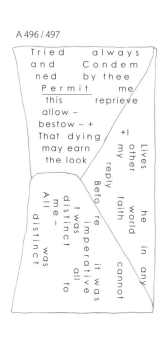

Tried   always
and   Condem
ned   by thee
Permit   me
this   reprieve
allow –
bestow – +
That dying
may earn
the look

+I

Lives   he in any
other   world
my   faith   cannot
reply

Befo re   it was
imperative   all
t was   to
distinct
me –
All   was
distinct
was
distinct

Tried almost
and Condemn
ned of the
Permit me
this reprieve
alum-
festering
that earth
may look
the look

gave

for which

I cease to

live —

A 496 / 497

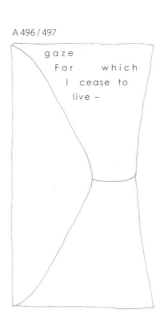

gaze
For   which
I cease to
live –

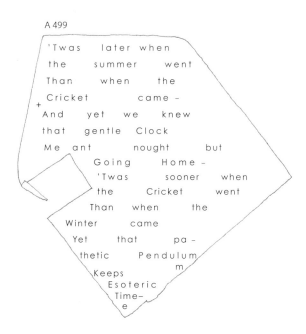

A 499

'Twas   later when
the   summer   went
Than   when   the
Cricket   came –
And   yet   we   knew
that   gentle Clock
Me ant   nought   but
Going   Home –
'Twas   sooner   when
the   Cricket   went
Than   when   the
Winter   came
Yet   that   pa –
thetic Pendulum
                m
Keeps
Esoteric
Time–
    e

'twas later when
the summer went
than when the
Cricket came -
And yet we knew
that gentle Clock
meant nought but
going Home -
'twas sooner when
the Cricket went
than when the
winter came
yet that pa-
thetic pendulum
keeps
esoteric
time

499

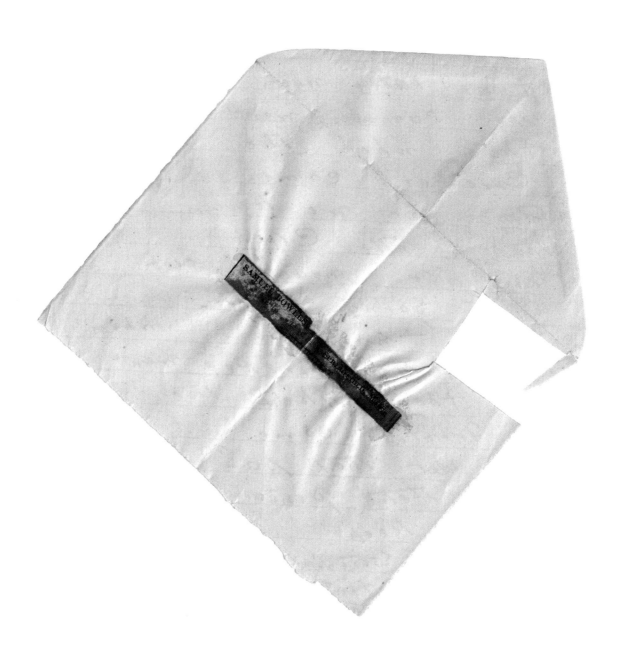

Miss Emily
Dickinson.

Amherst.
Mass.

PHILADELPHIA
NOV
24
10AM
PA.

514

We
talked with
each other
about each
other
though neither
of us spoke.
We were + too
engrossed with
the Second's Races
And the Hoofs of
the Clock.
Pausing in front
of our + sentenced
Faces
Time's Decision
shook.
Arks of Reprieve

+ were
listening
to the

+ foundering
Faces

time compas
sion took

he opened
to us.
Ararats.
we took.

102

A 514

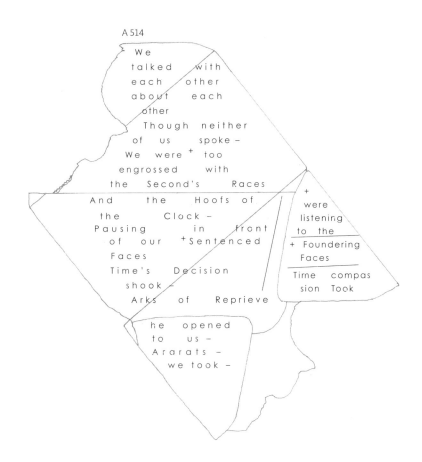

We
talked   with
each   other
about   each
other
    Though neither
of us   spoke –
We were ⁺ too
engrossed   with
the Second's   Races
And   the   Hoofs of   ⁺
the   Clock –   were
Pausing   in   front   listening
of our ⁺Sentenced   to the
Faces   ⁺ Foundering
Time's   Decision   Faces
shook –
Arks of   Reprieve   Time compas
                    sion Took
    he opened
to us –
Ararats –
we took –

A 531

Without   a   smile –
Without   a   Throe
+A   Summer's   soft
Assemblies   go
To   their   entrancing
end
Unknown –   for   all
the   times   we   met –
Estranged   , however
intimate –
What   a   dissembling
Friend –
+ Do –   our –
          Nature's   soft

531 Without a smile -
Without a throe
x A Summer's soft
Assemblies go
to their entrancing
end
Unknown - for all
the times we met -
Estranged however
intimate -
What a dissembling
friend -
+ no - our -
       Nature's soft

Mr. & Mrs. Edward Dickinson

A 539 / 539a

539

these are those
who are, shallow
intentionally,
and only
profound
by
accident—

A 539 / 539a

There are   those
who   are   shallow
intentionally
and   only
profound
by
accident

A 636 / 636a

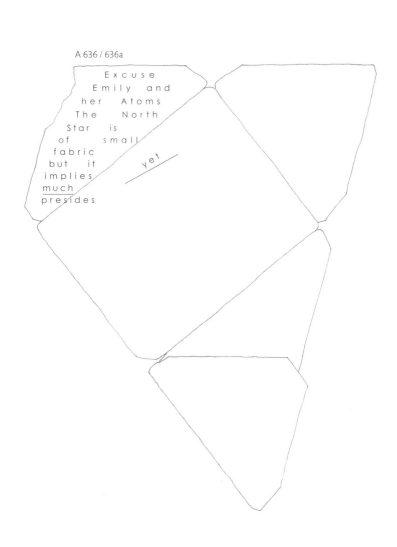

Excuse
Emily and
her Atoms
The North
Star is
of small
fabric
but it
implies
much
presides

yet

A 636 / 636a

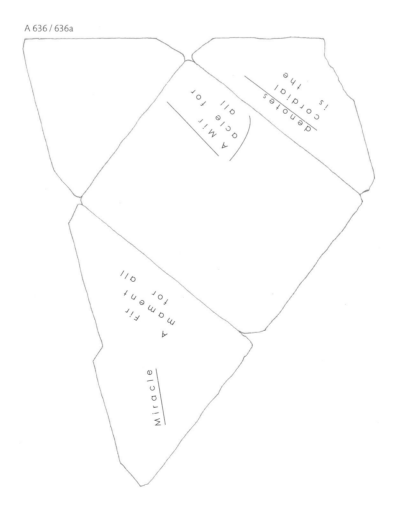

A 636 / 636a

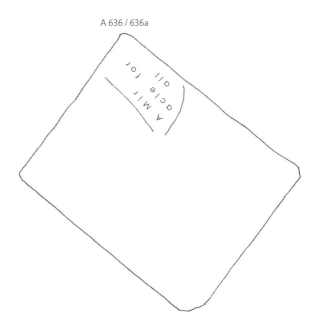

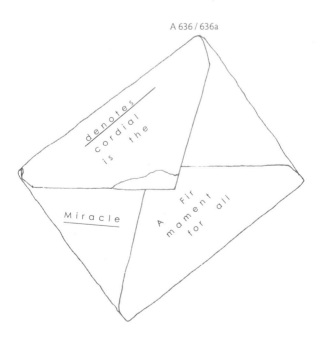

denotes
cordial   the
is

Miracle

A   Fir
mament
for   all

A 758 / 758a

Thank   you for
Knowing   I did
not   spurn   it,
because   it   was
   true   – I   did   not –
      refused
   I   denied   what   Mr
   Erskine   said   not
   from   detected   feeling
   but   of   myself
      it   was   not   true –
   I   ~~can not~~   suppose
      not   of   others

thank you for
knowing I did
not spurn it —
because it was
true — did not —
I denied what my
Erskine said not
even telling
others of myself —
it was not true
I cannot suppose
not of others

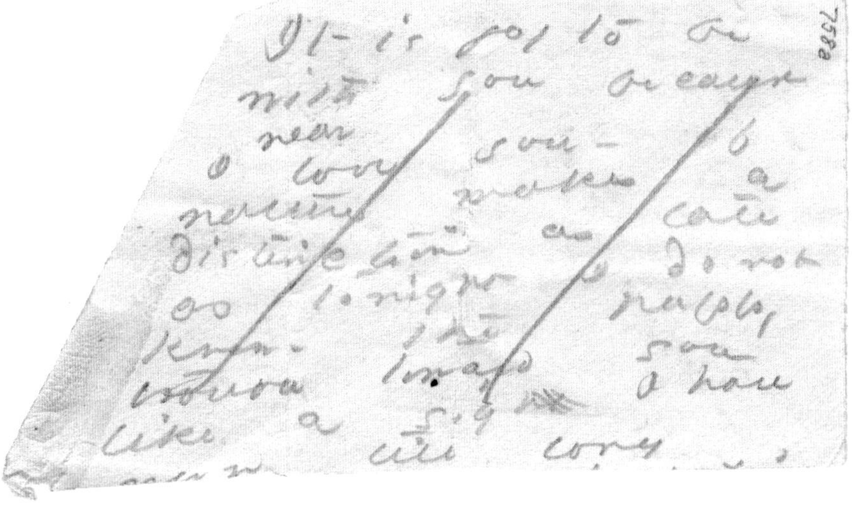
It is not to be
with you because
near
I long you – to
nothing makes a
distinction as call
so tonight I do not
know – the reach,
would lonely you
like a Sig I have
lies long
[illegible]
758a

A 758 / 758a

It   is   joy   to   be
with   you   because
near
I   love   you – it
nature   makes   a
distinction   as   late
as   tonight   I   do not
know –   the   happy
trouble   toward   you
like   a   sight   I have
till   long

A 821

Clogged
only with
Music, like
the Wheels of
Birds

their high
Appoint
ment

of
I

Afternoon and
the West and
the gorgeous
nothings
which
compose
the
sunset
keep

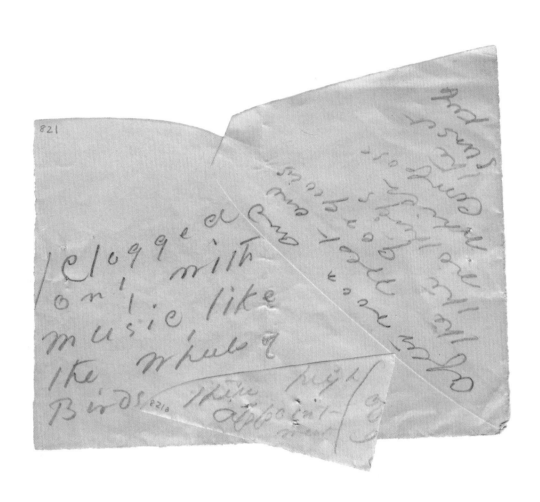

As there are
apartments in our
own minds that
we never enter
without Apology
we should respect
the bolts &
others

A 842

As there are
Apartments in our
own Minds that –
we never enter
without Apology –
we should respect
the seals of
others –

– which

A 843

But   are   not
all Facts   Dreams
as   soon   as
we   put
them   behind
us –

848 But are not
all facts. dreams
as soon as
we put
them behind
us.

844 But ought not the Amanuensis ~~also~~ to receive a Commission also.

A 844

But ought not the
Amanuensis ~~also~~ to
receive a Commission also –

A 857

I never saw
Mrs Jackson
but twice ,but
those twice are
indelible, and
one Day more
I am deified
was the only
impression she
Ever left on
Any House
Heart
she entered –

I never saw
Mrs. Jackson
but twice, but
those twice are
indelible, and
one Day more
I am deified —
was the only
impression she
ever left on
any House —
Heart
she entered —

Helen of Troy
will die, but
Helen of Colorado
nay.

Dear friend, can
you walk ? were
mere the last
words that
I wrote her

Dear friend
can fly – were
immortal –
soaring reply –

∧ 857

Helen   of   Troy
will   die,   but
Helen   of Colorado
never
Dear   friend, can
you   walk
were   the   last
words   that

I   wrote   her –
Dear   friend I
can   fly   –   her
   immortal
soaring   reply –

A 865

N o t   to s e n d
e r r a n d s   by J o h n
A l d e n   is
o n e   of the
i n s t r u c t i o n s
of

History –

865 not to send
errands by John
Alden is
one of the
instructions
of
History —

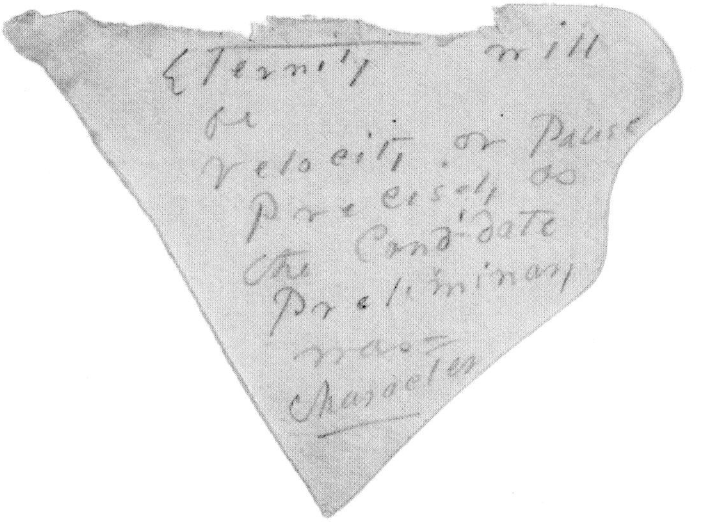

Eternity will
be
velocity or pause
precisely as
the Candidate
Preliminary
mast—
Character

HB3

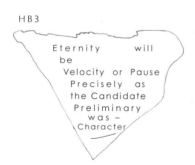

Eternity   will
be
Velocity or Pause
Precisely   as
the Candidate
Preliminary
was –
Character

Itineraries of Escape

Emily Dickinson's Envelope-Poems

Marta Werner

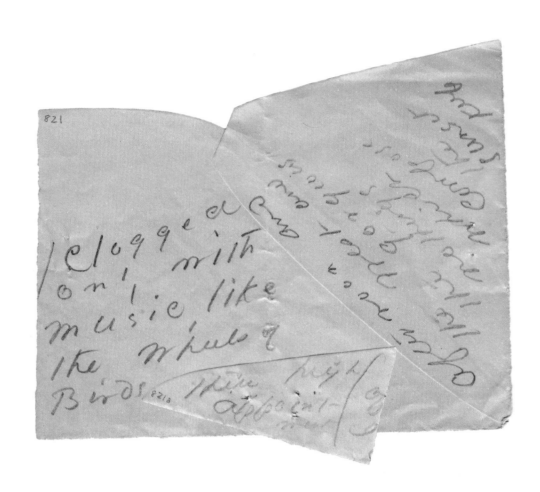

A 821, "Clogged | only with | Music, like | the Wheels of | Birds"

I.

"The Wheels of Birds"[1]

"Collections," write the editors of *Walter Benjamin's Archive*, "unlock themselves once a single piece is brought to voice. In the beginning was the exemplary object, which opens up the way to thought as if by itself. Groups of documents [arise from it]."[2] Among Emily Dickinson's last writings is such an exemplary manuscript. Identified solely by its catalog number, A 821, it constitutes a kind of exit text. It may have been composed in a few minutes, or even a few seconds, in the early spring of 1885, since one line of the text reappears, slightly altered, in three fair-copy drafts of a letter from Dickinson to Helen Hunt Jackson, composed around March of that year but apparently never completed or mailed. In Thomas H. Johnson and Theodora Ward's *The Letters of Emily Dickinson*, the envelope-poem is annexed to these drafts as a footnote. Its provenance, however, as well as the date of its composition, remains unconfirmed.

I found it by accident, in the Amherst College Library, when it fell (rose?) out of an acid-free envelope. If I had not held it lightly in my hands, I would never have suspected the manner in which it was assembled. Although its brevity and immediacy place it outside the reach of conventional classifications, it bears a striking affinity to the genre David Porter names "small, rickety infinitudes."[3]

Look at it here, flying on the page, vying with light.

Taxonomy of Paper Wings

A 821 is a sudden collage made of two sections of envelope.

The principles of its construction are economical, even austere. The larger section of the collage is the inside of the back of an envelope, the address face of which has been torn or cut away. One vertical crease bisects the document, turning the halved envelope into a simple diptych that resembles the hinged wings of the bird the holograph is becoming. Initially, the wings appear to have been folded, perhaps even pinned closed; at rest, the manuscript has yet to be transformed into a fully living figure. Another section of text is composed on an unfolded triangular corner of an envelope's seal; it has been designated by the cataloger "A 821a." A single straight pin, in place when I first found the manuscript, but since removed, originally imped—a verb from the vocabulary of falconry, when feathers are grafted into a bird's wing to restore or improve powers of flight—the collage elements together while also spreading open the larger envelope fragment to reveal the hidden visual rhyme of its wings and a blurred message about a sudden atmospheric convergence.

On the right wing, the lines "Afternoon and | the West and | the gorgeous | nothings | which | compose | the | sunset | keep" slant upward into the west.

On the left wing, the lines "Clogged | only with | Music, like | the Wheels of | Birds" slant diagonally upward into the east.

On the smaller, pinned wing, writing rushes beyond the tear or terminus where the visible meets the invisible in "their high | Appoint | ment."

The singing of birds marks—some even believe causes—both the break and the close of day.[4] If we read from left to right across the contours of the open wings, A 821 appears to record the moment when day falls into night. Yet the grammar—*syntax*—of wings is the grammar of discontinuity. The slight variations in the handwriting on opposing wings suggest that the texts they carry were composed on different occasions; moreover, on each wing, writing—inscribed by Velocity—rushes in opposite directions. To access the text(s), and to answer the question of where we have arrived, we must enter into a volitional relationship with the fragment, turning it point by point, like a compass or a pinwheel—like the *wheels of thought*. 360 degrees. As we rotate A 821, orienting and disorienting it at once, day and night—each a whir of words—almost collide in the missing spaces just beyond the light seams showing the bifurcation in the envelope, and then fly apart in a synesthesia of sight and sound.

Gravity Fields

"Joy | and Gravitation | have their own | ways –"[5]

The instantaneous translation from one condition into another, radically different one, defines the experience of Dickinson's late ecstatic writings. A 821 / 821a's textual status as a "fugitive" or "exile" is related not only to its extra-generic quality but also to its migration between and among texts and, finally, to its capacity to survive outside all the texts that briefly shelter it.

Even within the interstices of the letter-drafts that at first seem to repatriate and master the lyric fragment, A 821 marks the place where the amanuensis comes, slipping between registers in a voice at once immediate and alien, turning prose back into poetry. Initially though, the strange vibration of A 821 / 821a comes from a crossing of wires between Helen Hunt Jackson's 3 February 1885 letter to Dickinson containing news of her prolonged suffering from a broken leg and Dickinson's belated response in March of the same year:

Santa Monica | Cal. | By the Sea. | Feb. 3. 1885.

My dear Miss Dickinson,

Thank you heartily for the fan. It is pathetic, in its small-ness – poor souls – how did they come to think of making such tiny ones. – I shall wear it sometimes, like a leaf on my breast. –

Your letter found me in Los Angeles, where I have been for two months & a little more. – Sunning myself, and trying to get on my feet. – I had hoped by this time to be able to go without crutches, and venture to New York, for the remainder of the winter – but I am disappointed. So far as the broken leg is concerned, I could walk with a cane now: but the whole leg having been badly strained by doing double duty so long, is obstinate about getting to work again, is very lame and sore, & I am afraid badly given out – so that it will take months for it to recover. – I dislike this exceedingly; – but dare not grumble, lest a worse thing befall me: & if I did grumble, I should deserve it, – for I am absolutely well – drive the whole of every afternoon in an open carriage on roads where larks sing & flowers are in bloom: I can do everything I ever could – except walk! –

and if I never walk again it will still remain true that I have had more than a half century's excellent trotting out of my legs – so even then, I suppose I ought not be rebellious. – Few people get as much out of one pair of legs as I have! –

This Santa Monica is a lovely little Seaside hamlet, – only eighteen miles from Los Angeles, – one of the most beautiful Seaside places I ever saw: green to the *tip* edge of the cliffs, flowers blooming and choruses of birds, all winter. – There can be nothing in this world nearer perfection than this South California climate for winter. – Cool enough to make a fire necessary, night & morning: but warm enough to keep flowers going, all the time, in the open air, – grass & barley are many inches high – some of the "volunteer" crops already in head. – As I write – (in bed, before breakfast,) I am looking straight off towards Japan – over a silver sea – my foreground is a strip of high grass, and mallows, with a row of Eucalyptus trees sixty or seventy feet high: – and there is a positive cackle of linnets.

Searching here, for Indian relics, especially the mortars or bowls hollowed out of stone, with the solid stone pestles they used to pound their acorns in, I have found two Mexican women called *Ramona*, from whom I have bought the Indian mortars. –

I hope you are well – and at work – I wish I knew by now what your portfolios, by this time, hold.

Yours ever truly
Helen Jackson.[6]

The epistolary relation is grounded in and exposed to time. When Dickinson received her friend's letter, she began composing a response. Several drafts, here redacted into two by Thomas Johnson, remain extant:

draft no. 1

Dear friend –

    To reproach my own Foot in behalf of your's, is involuntary, and finding myself, no solace in "whom he loveth he chasteneth" your Valor astounds me. It was only a small Wasp, said the French Physician, repairing the sting, but the strength to perish is sometimes withheld, though who but you could tell a Foot.

    Take all away from me, but leave me Ecstasy
    And I am richer then, than all my Fellow Men.
    Is it becoming me to dwell so wealthily,
    When at my very Door are those possessing more,
    In abject Poverty?

    That you compass "Japan" before you breakfast, not in the least surprises me, clogged only with Music, like the Wheels of Birds.
    Thank you for hoping I am well. Who could be ill in March, that month of proclamation? Sleigh Bells and Jays contend in my Matinee, and the North surrenders, instead of the South, a reverse of Bugles.
    Pity me, however, I have finished Ramona.
    Would that like Shakespeare, it were just published! Knew I how to pray, to intercede for your Foot were intuitive – but I am but a Pagan –

    Of God we ask one favor,
    That we may be forgiven –

draft no. 2

Dear friend –

    To reproach my own foot in behalf of your's, is involuntary, and finding meager solace in "whom he chasteneth," your prowess astounds me. It was only a small Wasp, said the french physician repairing the sting, but the [   ] tell a foot.

Take all away from me, but leave me Ecstasy
And I am richer then I am [   ]

strength to perish is sometimes withheld, yet who but you can [   ] tell a
Foot.

Take all away from me, but leave me Ecstasy,
And I am richer then, than all my Fellowmen.
Is it becoming me to dwell so wealthily,
When at my very Door are those possessing more,
In abject poverty.

But the strength to perish is sometimes withheld.

That you glance at Japan as you breakfast, not in the least surprises me,
thronged only with Music, like the Decks of Birds. Thank you for hoping
I am well. Who could be ill in March, that Month of proclamation? Sleigh
Bells and Jays contend in my Matinee, and the North surrenders instead of
the South, a reverse of Bugles. Pity me, however, I have finished Ramona.

Would that like Shakespeare, it were just published! Knew I how to
pray, to intercede for your Foot were intuitive, but I am but a Pagan.

Of God we ask one favor,
That we may be forgiven –
For what, he is presumed to know –
The Crime, from us, is hidden –
Immured the whole of Life
Within a magic Prison
We reprimand the Happiness
That too competes with Heaven –

May I once more know, and that you are saved?

Your Dickinson[7]

Dickinson *was* writing. She had even signed one draft. Perhaps she was nearly ready to seal a final version into an envelope and speed it on its way. But before she could make these final preparations, the newspapers announced Jackson's death. Dickinson's carefully drafted response to Jackson's morning letter reaches its destination only in the night of its intended recipient.[8]

Unlike the letter proper, a narrative of illness and death, boundlessly gravid, the undated because dateless fragment is a site of radical temporality.

In the visual linguistics of early mystical imagery and Edenic metaphysics, wings / wheels are signifiers for immateriality, for bodies that are not subject to the laws of gravity. Wings / wheels can communicate between time and eternity.[9] By composing A 821 / A 821a on the reverse of an empty, unaddressed envelope, no longer the container for a message, but the message itself, Dickinson creates a template for flight that is also a trope for her late, contrapuntal communications, in which "arrival" is another name for "departure."

In examining the body of A 821 / 821a still more closely, four additional sets of pinpricks, two along the outer edges of the left wing, and two along the outer edges of the right wing, are revealed. These tiny holes may be signs that the fragment was imped to other texts composed and circulated before or after the letter to Hunt Jackson, signs that writing is subject to changes in course, to multiple defections.

Pinned, unpinned, and repinned, the fragment's flights shatter the deep, one-point perspective of the letter and keep the texts / birds flying in a splintered mode of time, in the "terrifying tense" of pure transition.[10] A 821 / 821a may be a poem-breaking-out-of-prose, a time-shifted bird flown out of the constellation of March, a translation of speed or spirit into a kind of handwriting, a dart that returns immediately to the sender. In such a case, the expectations of closure or parousia—"their high | Appoint | ment"—may be endlessly postponed or reversed by the drop of a pin.

To say the least, the common meter of the hymn so often evident in Dickinson's early bound poems has not survived this latest flight. In A 821 / 821a, a sudden acceleration is followed by the snapping or short-circuiting of lyrical cables. In place of melody and measure come suddenness and syncope: "meter with neither more or less, but an impossible measure."[11] A 821 / 821a flies to the outermost edges of Dickinson's oeuvre, then out of this world.

"No Bird – but rode in Ether –"[12]

The direction in which the fragment is heading is further clarified in August (perhaps) of 1885, when on what appear to be postal wrappers, Dickinson composed the following ex-static postscript to Hunt Jackson: "Dear friend, can | you walk | were the last | words that | I wrote her – | Dear friend I | can fly – her | immortal | soaring reply –" (A 857 / 857a).[13]

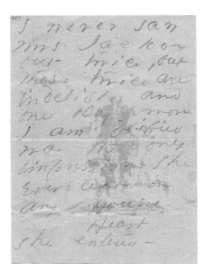

A 857, "I never saw | Mrs Jackson"

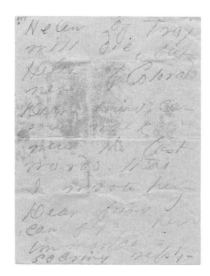

A 857a, "Helen of Troy | will die, but"

II.

A Further Migration

"W. H. Hudson says that birds feel something akin to pain
(and fear) just before migration and that nothing alleviates
this feeling except flight (the rapid motion of wings)."[14]
            —Lorine Niedecker

A certain set of operations, repeated again and again, like the rapid motions
of wings, may signify that a greater migration is already underway.

A 821 / 821a comes not alone but as one migrant among many. It is the
harbinger, moreover, of Dickinson's furthest flight—beyond the forty bound
fascicles, the accumulated libraries of her poetic production—into a freer air
where, to cite her contemporary, Ralph Waldo Emerson, "contrary and remote
things [seem to] cohere."[15] At this juncture Dickinson no longer thinks of keeping
what she acquires through the labor of writing, and her attitude of astonishing
recklessness is reflected in her new practice of writing on anything and everything
near to hand: chocolate wrappers, the margins of books, scraps of paper...

Among the many makeshift and fragile textual homes for Dickinson's late
writings we find the fifty-two envelopes gathered here. The nature of Dickinson's
connection to these works remains obscure. For while it is unlikely that she set
out to record a series of poems, messages, and fragments on envelopes, once we
have seen these documents, it becomes difficult to dissociate the texts from their
carriers. Flocked together for a few moments before dispersing again into other
equally provisional constellations, they remind us that a writer's archive is not a
storehouse of easily inventoried contents—i.e., "poems," "letters," etc.—but also a
reservoir of ephemeral remains, bibliographical escapes.

Like so many of Dickinson's writings, the fifty-two envelope-texts
discovered in an initial sweep of the major collections of her manuscripts often
vex genre boundaries. Most, however, appear to be rough-copy poems or the
lyric beginnings or endings of poems. The earliest "envelope-poem" may have
been composed around 1864, the date Ralph W. Franklin assigns to the last of
Dickinson's bound fascicles, and a handful of other envelope-texts—four by
Thomas H. Johnson's dating, two by Franklin's—belong to the same decade. The

remaining envelope-poems bear composition dates ranging from 1870 to 1885, evidence, perhaps, that Dickinson's practice of composing on envelopes intensified in the wake of fascicle production and at the juncture when she was testing, differently, and for a final time, the relationship between message and medium.[16]

Composed, too, at the end of a century whose "dream of communication as the mutual communion of souls"[17] was often realized or shattered by the fate of written messages, Dickinson's envelope poems seem charged with a special poignancy and hermeneutical burden. Unlike the original communications they may once have enclosed, the "emptied" envelopes discovered among Dickinson's papers after her death are scattered to the winds of the future, addressed to no one and everyone at once. Intercepted as they are by unknown and invisible readers permanently estranged from the writer, they remind us of the contingency, transience, vulnerability, and *hope* embodied in all our messages.

A 450, "The way | Hope builds his | House"

Dickinson lived and wrote at the very historical moment when the possibility of delivering through the modern postal system a private message to a specific addressee was first realized: "By the late 1850s," writes media historian John Durham Peters, "it was possible to mail a letter sealed in an envelope, paid for with a pre-purchased stamp, and dropped into a public box."[19] And in her recent work on Dickinson, Virginia Jackson considers the many possible forms and figures of address: "The way in which I address you depends upon where you are. If you are very near, I can whisper. If you are across the table, I can speak. If you are upstairs or just outside, I can shout. If you are too distant to hear (even to overhear) my voice, I can write. And in the illusion peculiar to written address, the condition of your absence (the condition of my writing) conjures a presence more intimate than a whisper."[20]

Before bearing poems, the envelopes found among Dickinson's papers presumably carried such cloistered dispatches. Of these, some that she later turned back into drafting spaces were originally addressed to her or to members of her family by persons in the world beyond the Homestead. The hands of her Norcross cousins, Josiah and Elizabeth Holland, Abigail Cooper, Judge Otis Lord, and Helen Hunt Jackson, among others, inked them, affixed the requisite stamps, and committed them to the postal service.

A 479

The remaining envelopes are addressed by Dickinson to cherished outsiders. Unlike the envelopes mailed to her by others, these almost always bear only a name and, on rare occasion, an abbreviated address. Like Dickinson's untitled and undated poems, which circulated outside the conditions of print and the economy of technical reproduction, the original messages these envelopes presumably enclosed eluded the postal system's public circuits of exchange and were conveyed, if at all, by more intimate, now anonymous carriers. Neither stamped nor postmarked, their histories of transmission and reception are often impossible to trace (A 313 / 314).

A 313 / 314

"Returning is a different route,"[21] Dickinson wrote around 1874. If the envelopes addressed by Dickinson to others relayed communications received but long since dissociated from their covers and lost or destroyed according to custom or chance, why and by what path or agent did the empty casings come back to her? If, as may also be possible, these envelopes never left her possession, why did she address them at all? Were they only the potential carriers for missives Dickinson intended to write or wrote but in the end reserved? Could the poems inscribed on envelopes—both those unsent (or returned) to her and those sent to her by others—be the true messages she wished to transmit but never did? To whom were they directed—to the living or to the dead?

There is a striking contrast between the address Dickinson inscribed on the envelope's face in ink and the poem she composed in pencil on its back or slit-open inside. This contrast corresponds in part to a split intention in the writer. The addresses appear in a magnified fair-copy script, and mark Dickinson's wish to send an indelible message to a singular addressee still present and locatable in the world; the poems, on the other hand, scrawled in the small, dense rough-copy script that Higginson said looked like the fossil-tracks of birds,[22] mark her desire to compose a fleeting message to a stranger from another, unknown world (A 105a).

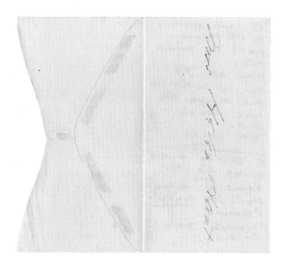
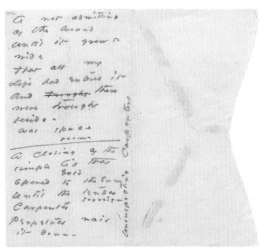

A 105

A 105a, "A not admitting | of the Wound"

How can we ever verify the degree to which what is transmitted matches what is received?

The interval separating address and poem—whether minutes, hours, days, or years—is indeterminate and may be(come) infinite.

Thus while it is tempting to see the poems composed on envelopes addressed to the same person as installments of some extended message to him or her—to see the addressee enciphered in the poems—the fragmentary narratives that emerge from such an approach often remain frustratingly unconnected to identifiable circumstances in the lives of either sender or recipient. What is renounced in the turning of the envelope from front to back is the letter's—the poem's—potential to conjure the addressee's presence through words: *Even when I hold your letter in my hands, I am not touching you.* This very same turn affirms the mysterious distance separating the sender and receiver even as they nonetheless continue to signal to each other.

A message enclosed in an envelope, a poem inscribed upon it and prepared for sending over miles or years is not a bit or byte of information but an archive of longings. No wonder, then, that we find among Dickinson's envelope-poems several enacting the ecstatic reconciliation of souls. "Long Years | apart – can | make no | Breach a | second cannot | fill –" (A 277), for example, asserts the power of writing to overcome time and space, to collapse the distance dividing writer and addressee, who then recognize each other instantaneously despite revolutions in time.

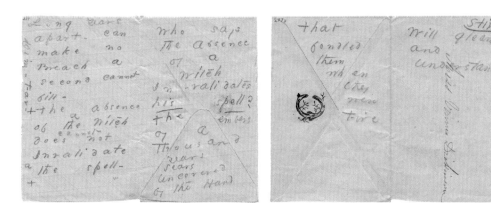

A 277 and A 277a, "Long Years | apart – can"

This fantasy, however, recurs only rarely in Dickinson's work. Far more often, the envelope-poems emphasize the "address gap,"[23] depict the vast "expanse" sundering writer and reader, so often also lover and beloved. As if we needed reminding, Jerome A. Miller writes, "All the beings toward which wonder draws us are themselves drawn irretrievably toward nothingness."[24] And so, in "Through what | transports of | Patience" (A 479) comes the recognition that the addressee is unreachable, separated from the writer who seeks him or her by a void or "Blank" that, not measurable by human scales, can never be traversed in this world.

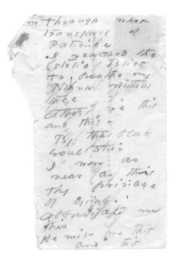

A 479, "Through what | transports of | Patience"

Similarly, the brief but excruciating poem "A not admitting | of the Wound" (A 105a)—in which we learn only that the source of the speaker's injury is her severance from the beloved and that the wound is so wide that her entire existence has now been consumed by it—bears witness to the anguish that attends our perception of what Emerson so long ago recognized as the "infinite remoteness"[25] of our condition. In this case, the translation of the wound into words remains unaccompanied by an interpretive process that might help cure the speaker by turning her literal hurt into a figurative one. The envelope is the repository of damages it cannot heal or even contain: slit open, it functions not as a soothing bandage, but, rather, as a second and almost simultaneous site of rupture.

"What a | Hazard | a Letter | is —"[26] Dickinson scrawled in a late fragment composed in a handwriting so disordered it seems to have been formed in the dark. Just when we least suspect the arrow is aimed for us, we are "letterstruck."[27] Thus on the back of another envelope stored or abandoned among Dickinson's papers, its cover nearly translucent, its tendril-like address penned in a watery blue-lavender, we find a summons to the end of the world. The luxurious slowness of the message's passage over the terrain of the nineteenth century by train or carriage cannot defer the suddenness with which we receive it:

A 165, "Death warrants are | supposed to be"

"Speed" was to be Dickinson's watchword. She lived and wrote in the century of suddenness, amid the rise of new telecommunications technologies that altered forever the forms of human contact: "The new media," writes Durham Peters, "gave life to the older dream of angelic contact by claiming to burst the bonds of distance and death."[28] Yet they also delivered us into new solitudes. One of the uncanniest documents in the constellation of Dickinson's writings on envelopes is a Western Union telegraph blank addressed to Vinnie Dickenson [*sic*], Care of Judge Lord, and marked "paid" by the sender. The urgent message it conveyed—copied by a nameless telegrapher with strict instructions to "carefully read… every letter," to repeat "obscure sentence[s] or difficult word[s]," and to "keep a daily record of all difficulties, interruptions or incidents occurring in the working of lines"[29]—has vanished. Yet in the poems that take its place, "Glass was | the Street – | in Tinsel | Peril" and "It came his | turn to beg –" (see A 193 / 194), Dickinson appears to be translating the electrical pulses of the original and unrecoverable bulletin into new messages associating swiftness with shock. The breakdown and cancelation of the final words and phrases of these dictations to Dickinson by someone or thing from the Outside appear as verification that the simultaneous communion between minds—or even between the mind that thinks and the hand that writes—is not achievable. Transmissions in this world are asymmetrical and full of gaps. We receive and decipher them only ever in parts.

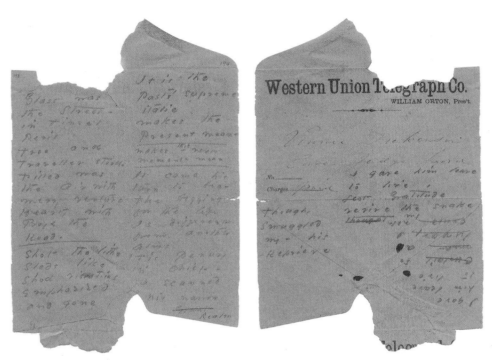

A 193 / 194, "Glass was | the Street –"

"*Springs – shake the seals – *"[30]

Among Dickinson's envelope-poems we find an exquisite subset of lyric fragments written on seals or flaps. Disconnected from their original bodies, the seals compose a coda for all of Dickinson's late writings received in pieces, as fragments.

The tiny scale and luminous properties of the seal link it to the world of the miniature—to the keepsake or amulet. In writing, the seal is the ideal container for the aphorism: a minimum sign invested with a maximal energy.[31] Only a few lines long, the poems inscribed over seals bear witness to the evanescence of existence, brief as a single day or as the isolate, piercing notes of a bird. Saved against all odds, unsealed for all the world to see, they carry Dickinson's last, exorbitant message about fame's "siteless[ness]," and her final—cancelled—caution against doubt.

A 252, "In this short Life"

A 320, "One note from | One Bird"

A 539a, "There are those | who are shallow"

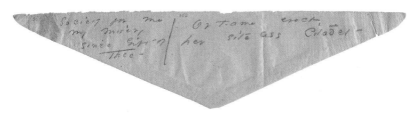

A 351 / 352, "Society for me | my misery" / "Or Fame erect | her siteless Citadel –"

A 449, "The vastest Earthly Day"

One of the nineteenth-century words for envelope was "cover," and envelopes are metaphors of containment, of exteriority and interiority, of enfolding and exposure. In Dickinson's case, however, the sovereign force of the envelopes' addresses, with their promise of exclusivity, is ultimately countered by the poems' openness to a multiplicity of recipients, an array of futures. The inaudible *whirring* of the envelopes is part of the message they are sending. Slit open, unfolded, written across, and handed over to chance, they reject the asylum offered by the lyric to probe the last privacies of our existence.

"Tuning the Sky"[32]: *Scatter Diagrams*

"High up, a mile high, perhaps two miles high, hundreds…of pale
grey birds flew south, like pages of flickering paper let loose from
a small book caught up in a wind…"[33]

—Peter Greenaway

"Distance – be her only | + Signal – "[34]

—Emily Dickinson

Before closing, one final glimpse of A 821, flying on the page, vying for light.

A 821, "Clogged | only with | Music, like | the Wheels of | Birds"

In order to determine whether or not certain kinds of birds possess homing
instincts, a person known as a "liberator" throws several up into the air, then turns
and turns again, each time releasing more birds in different directions. The birds
are then watched out of sight and the points at which they disappear from view
are recorded. When a significant number of vanishing points has been noted, a
"scatter diagram" is drawn up for study. At times, for reasons poorly understood,
large numbers of birds seem to lose their way back to their original release point
and drift widely across the migration access.[35]

Beyond the fascicles, beyond even Dickinson's writing desk and the room it
occupies, the air is filling with her papers. Circling the absent center of the book,

218

Dickinson's envelope-poems resemble the distant migrants that do not come fully into focus and so never constitute a clearly delimitable constellation. The wind moves them. Time moves them. If, in a given moment, one or two seem to be in close touch, each in the next moment seems remote from the others, unassimilable to a larger figure, whose moving edges drift and blur. More importantly, perhaps, like the homing birds gone astray, they have exchanged the hermetic relations inherent in letters, those "fine and private things" sent to one intimate and elite addressee, for the more elliptical but finally more far-reaching relations of poems. Although they may never have left her papers, Dickinson's envelope-writings are still en route, their itinerary open. Their meanings or messages, dispersed to all, free of instructions, may be fleetingly intercepted by anyone with eyes to see, with ears to hear.

Instead of classifying the envelope-writings according to conventional bibliographical codes, we need to find ways of launching them into circulation again and again. Ideally, the reader of these writings will assume the role of "liberator," releasing them high up into the ether, following them until they are out of sight, noting their vanishing points, and, whenever possible, replying to them, counting each brief connection with them as an instant of grace.

Notes

1. This Emily Dickinson fragment, A 821, is housed in the Amherst College Library, Archives & Special Collections. For published sources, see *The Letters of Emily Dickinson*, 3 vols., edited by Thomas H. Johnson, with Theodora Ward (Cambridge, MA: The Belknap Press of Harvard University Press, 1958), L976n, and *Radical Scatters: An Electronic Archive of Emily Dickinson's Late Fragments and Related Texts, 1870–1886*, edited by Marta L. Werner (Lincoln, NE: Center for Digital Research in the Humanities, 2011): http://libxml1a.unl.edu/8080/cocoon/radicalscatters/default-login.html.

2. Ursula Marx et al., *Walter Benjamin's Archive: Images, Texts, Signs*, translated by Esther Leslie (London: Verso, 2007), 4.

3. David Porter, "Assembling a Poet and Her Poems: Convergent Limit-Works of Joseph Cornell and Emily Dickinson." *Word & Image* 10:3 (1994): 199.

4. See Leonard Lutwack, *Birds in Literature* (Gainesville, FL: University of Florida Press, 1994).

5. This line is drawn from another fragment, A 871, found among Dickinson's papers after her death and now housed in the Amherst College Library, Archives & Special Collections. For published sources, see *The Letters of Emily Dickinson*, PF44, and *Radical Scatters*.

6. *The Letters of Emily Dickinson*, L976a.

7. *The Letters of Emily Dickinson*, L976. Thomas H. Johnson's transcription is a redaction of three manuscript drafts found among Dickinson's papers after her death and now housed in the Amherst College Library, Archives & Special Collections: A 817, A 818, and A 819. In addition to the three letter-drafts associated with this text, two fragments—A 820 and A 822—are also part of the same constellation, A 817–A 822. For facsimiles of these associated documents, see *Radical Scatters*.

8. On August 6, 1885, the *Springfield Republican* noted, "Mrs. Jackson is reported at the point of death in San Francisco, where she has been steadily declining for the last four months." She died six days later, on August 12. In a letter to Thomas Wentworth Higginson, Dickinson wrote, "I was unspeakably shocked to see this in the Morning Paper – She wrote me in Spring that she could not walk, but not that she would die – I was sure you would know. Please say it is not so. What a Hazard a Letter is! When I think of the Hearts it has scuttled and sunk, I almost fear to lift my Hand to so much as a Superscription. Trusting that all is peace in your loved Abode, With alarm, Your Scholar – ." See *The Letters of Emily Dickinson*, L1007.

9. See, for example, the extended exploration of flight iconography and iconology in Clive Hart, *Images of Flight* (Berkeley, CA: University of California Press, 1988). See also Marina Warner, *The Inner Eye: Art Beyond the Visible* (London: National Touring Exhibitions, 1996).

10. I have appropriated the phrase "terrifying tense" from Leslie Scalapino's "Objects in the Terrifying Tense / Longing from Taking Place," in *A Poetics of Criticism*, eds. Juliana Spahr et al. (Buffalo, NY: Leave Books, 1994), 37.

11. See Catherine Clément, *Syncope: The Philosophy of Rapture*, translated by Sally O'Driscoll and Dierdre M. Mahoney (Minneapolis, MN: University of Minnesota Press, 1994). See also Michael Pierssens, "Detachment," *New York Literary Forum* 8–9 (1981): 166.

12. This line is drawn from the draft of a letter Dickinson composed to an unknown addressee identified only as "Master." The draft, A 828, is currently housed in the Amherst College Library, Archives & Special Collections. For a facsimile of the manuscript, see *The Master Letters of Emily Dickinson*, edited by R. W. Franklin (Amherst, MA: Amherst College Press, 1986), 44–45.

13. The manuscript from which these lines were drawn, A 857, is a rough-copy draft found among Dickinson's papers after her death and currently housed in the Amherst College Library, Archives & Special Collections. Thomas H. Johnson printed the text in *The Letters of Emily Dickinson*, L1015. Johnson's suggestion that the draft was destined for William Jackson, Helen Hunt Jackson's widowed husband, is possible but not likely: Dickinson wrote to Jackson only once, and this letter was a message of condolence sent in mid-August 1885 (see *Letters*, L1009).

14. The quotation attributed to Lorine Niedecker is from a letter dated January 30, 1968; see Lisa Pater Faranda, ed., *"Between Your House and Mine": The Letters of Lorine Niedecker to Cid Corman, 1960–1970* (Durham, NC: Duke University Press, 1986), 149.

15. Ralph Waldo Emerson, "The American Scholar," in *Nature; Addresses and Lectures*, 1849. Reprinted in *Emerson: Essays and Lectures* (New York, NY: Library of America), 1983.

16. It is also possible that Dickinson used envelopes as drafting spaces at other, earlier times, and that these worksheet drafts have been destroyed. If so, Dickinson's attitude toward the envelope-poems seems to undergo a change post fascicle production: the late envelope-texts were saved even when other fair copies exist.

17. John Durham Peters, *Speaking Into the Air: A History of the Idea of Communication* (Chicago, IL: University of Chicago Press, 1999), 1. Although Dickinson is nowhere cited in this work, Peters' beautifully conceived and deeply compelling study addresses her writings in countless ways.

18. These lines open Emily Dickinson's "Reportless Subjects, to | the Quick," which appears on an unbound sheet (A 88-17/18) housed in the Amherst College Library, Archives & Special Collections, and published in R. W. Franklin's *The Manuscript Books of Emily Dickinson*, 2 vols. (Cambridge, MA: The Belknap Press of Harvard University Press, 1981), Set 6a, p. 1090.

19. Peters, *Speaking Into the Air*, 166.

20. Virginia Jackson, *Dickinson's Misery: A Theory of Lyric Reading* (Princeton, NJ: Princeton University Press, 2005), 133.

21. This line appears in Emily Dickinson's poem beginning "No man saw awe, nor to." The holograph of this poem is not extant, though a variant fragment (A 295) found among Dickinson's papers after her death and currently housed in the Amherst College Library, Archives & Special Collections, rumors its existence. For a copy of the lost poem transcribed by Mabel Loomis Todd from the lost manuscript, see *The Poems of Emily Dickinson: A Variorum Edition*, P1342; for manuscript facsimiles of Dickinson's fragment and Todd's transcript of the lost poem, see *Radical Scatters*.

22. Thomas Wentworth Higginson, *The Magnificent Activist: The Writings of Thomas Wentworth Higginson, 1823–1911*, edited by Howard N. Mayer (Cambridge, MA: Da Capo Press, 2000), 544.

23. See Herbert Menzel, "Quasi-Mass Communication: A Neglected Area." *Public Opinion Quarterly* 35 (1971): 406–9. Menzel's concept of the "address gap" resonates strongly with Paul Ricoeur's notion of "distantiation"; see his *Hermeneutics and the Human Sciences: Essays on Language, Action, and Interpretation*, translated by John B. Thompson (Cambridge: Cambridge University Press, 1981).

24. Jerome A. Miller, *In the Throe of Wonder: Intimations of the Sacred in a Post-Modern World* (Albany, NY: State University of New York Press, 1992), 183.

25. Ralph Waldo Emerson, "Friendship," in *Essays: First Series* 1841 (Charlottesville, VA: Electronic Text Center, The University of Virginia Library, 1995): http://etext.virginia.edu/toc/modeng/public/EmeEssF.html.

26. This line is drawn from a Dickinson fragment (A 809) found among her papers after her death and currently housed in the Amherst College Library, Archives & Special Collections. The fragment, dated "about 1885" by Thomas H. Johnson, was composed by Dickinson on a torn remnant of a book dust jacket. The full text reads as follows: "What a | Hazard | a Letter | is – When | I think of | the Hearts | it has | Cleft | or healed I | almost | wince to | lift my Hand | to so much | as as a | superscription | but then we | always Ex | cept | ourselves – [verso] or | Scuttled and | Sunk." Three additional documents belong to the same textual constellation: A 802, a variant fragment; BPL Higg 116, a letter to Thomas Wentworth Higginson, commenting on Hunt Jackson's death; and the Oresman manuscript, a letter, possibly to Sara Colton (Gillett). For published sources, see *The Letters of Emily Dickinson*, L1007, L1007n, L1011, L1011n; and *Radical Scatters*.

27. The word "letterstruck" is Helene Cixous's — or at least a translation of her original French word. It appears in her exquisite essay, "Bathsheba or the interior Bible," translated by Catherine A F. MacGillivray, and collected in Cixous's *Stigmata: Escaping Texts* (London and New York: Routledge Press, 1998), 11.

28. Peters, *Speaking Into the Air*, 142.

29. These lines issue from an official manual from the *Western Union Telegraph Rules* (1866). The full text of the manual is available online: http://www.civilwarsignals.org/pages/

tele/wurules1866/wurules.html; the passages cited appear in Rules 8, 38, and 37, respectively.

30. This line appears in one of the many revisions (Franklin, revision d) of Dickinson's poem beginning "Safe in their Alabaster chambers" (H 203). See also R. W. Franklin's reconstruction of the history of this poem's composition in *The Poems of Emily Dickinson* (Cambridge, MA: The Belknap Press of Harvard University Press, 1998), P124, versions a–g.

31. For a splendid reading of the miniature, see Susan Stewart, *On Longing: Narratives of the Miniature, the Gigantic, the Souvenir, the Collection* (Durham, NC, and London: Duke University Press, 1993).

32. Susan Howe, *Defenestration of Prague* (New York: The Kulchur Foundation, 1983), 9.

33. Peter Greenaway, *Flying Out of this World* (Chicago: University of Chicago Press, 1994), 149.

34. A variant line in Dickinson's poem beginning "Her Sweet turn to leave." See *The Manuscript Books of Emily Dickinson*, vol. 2, Fascicle 34, pp. 817–19.

35. See G. V. T. Matthews, *Bird Navigation* (Cambridge: Cambridge University Press, 1968), 49.

Visual Index

Jen Bervin

Index of Envelopes by Page Shape

FLAPS AND SEALS

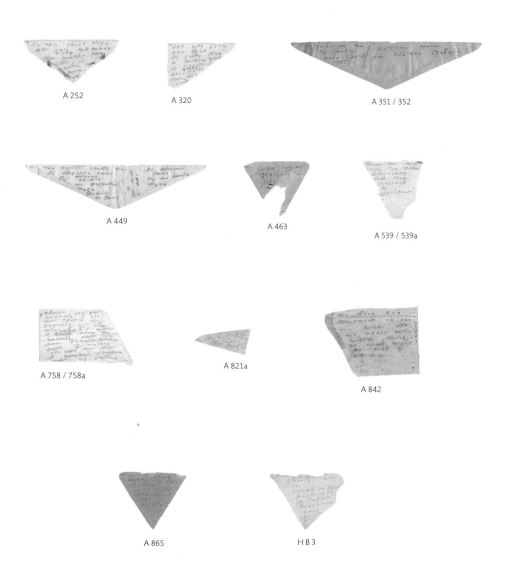

A 252

A 320

A 351 / 352

A 449

A 463

A 539 / 539a

A 758 / 758a

A 821a

A 842

A 865

H B 3

ARROWS

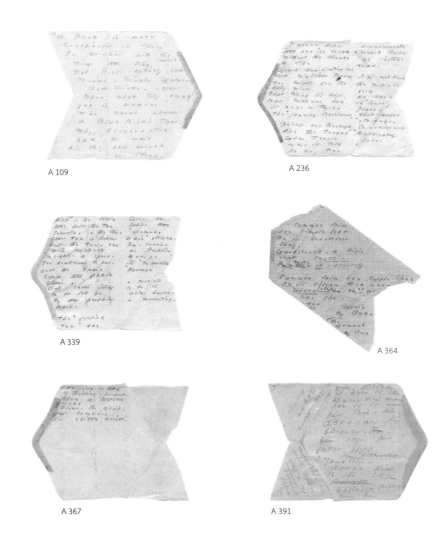

A 109

A 236

A 339

A 364

A 367

A 391

POINTLESS ARROWS

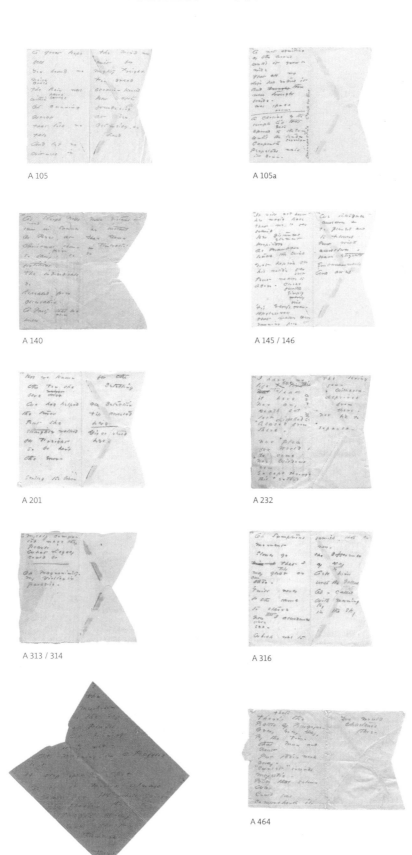

A 105

A 105a

A 140

A 145 / 146

A 201

A 232

A 313 / 314

A 316

A 416

A 464

Index of Envelopes by Address

ENVELOPES ADDRESSED BY EMILY DICKINSON

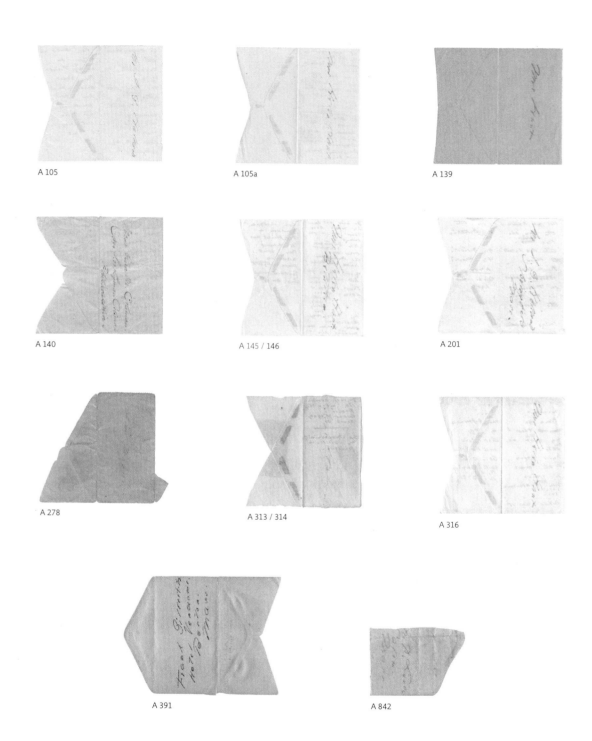

A 105

A 105a

A 139

A 140

A 145 / 146

A 201

A 278

A 313 / 314

A 316

A 391

A 842

Index of Envelopes by Address

Lavinia Dickinson

A 202

A 236

A 339

A 367

Frances Norcross

A 128

A 464

Louise Norcross

A 108

Josiah Gilbert Holland

A 232

Abigail Cooper

A 277

Clara Newman Turner

A 165

Edward Dickinson

A 438

Otis Lord

A 479

A 636 / 636a

A 105

A 108

A 139

A 140

A 145 / 146

A 193 / 194

A 201

A 232

A 236

A 277

A 316

A 332

A 339

A 438

A 464

A 488

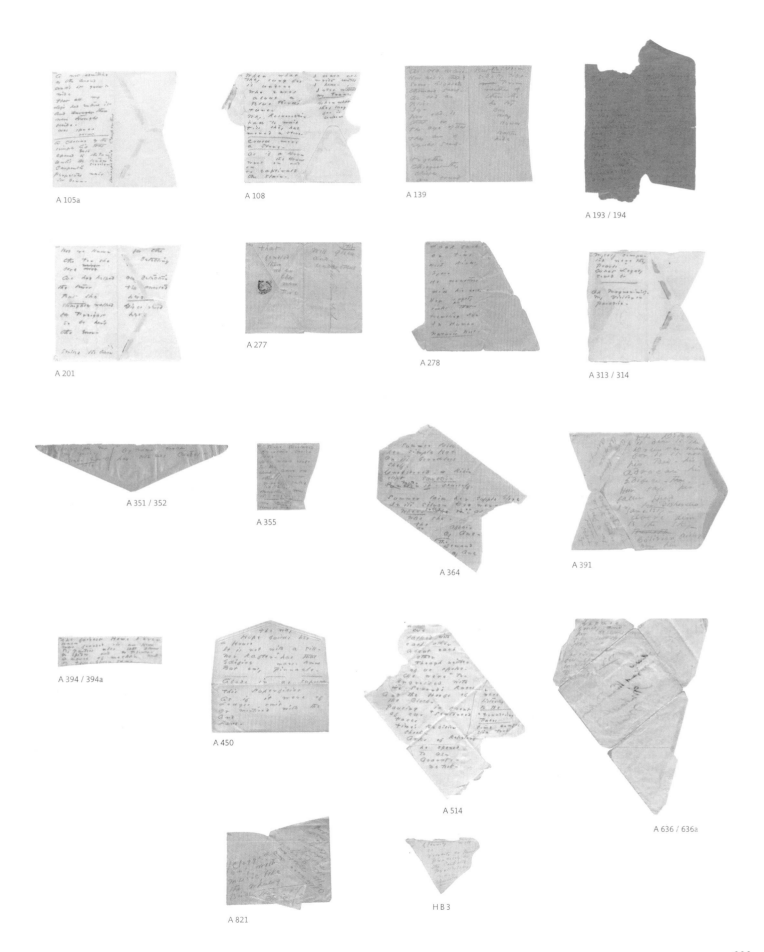

A 105a

A 108

A 139

A 193 / 194

A 201

A 277

A 278

A 313 / 314

A 351 / 352

A 355

A 364

A 391

A 394 / 394a

A 450

A 514

A 636 / 636a

A 821

HB 3

Index of Envelopes with Multidirectional Text

A 105a

A 165

A 193 / 194

A 232

A 277

Λ 332

A 391

A 438

A 449

A 488

A 496 / 497

A 636 / 636a

A 821

A 842

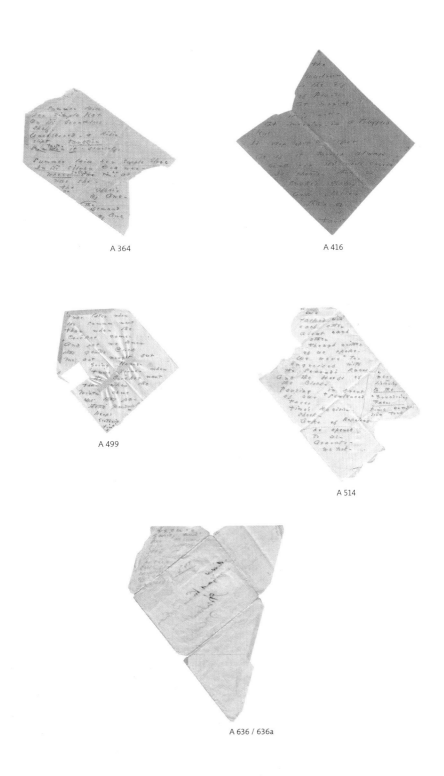

A 364

A 416

A 499

A 514

A 636 / 636a

Index of Envelopes with Cancelled or Erased Text

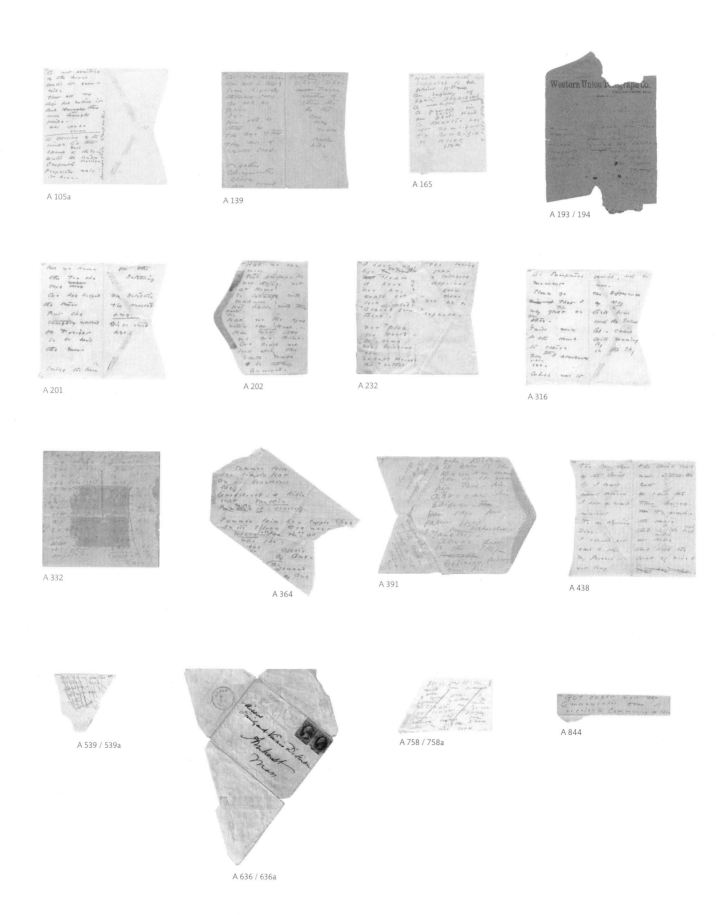

A 105a

A 139

A 165

A 193 / 194

A 201

A 202

A 232

A 316

A 332

A 364

A 391

A 438

A 539 / 539a

A 636 / 636a

A 758 / 758a

A 844

Index of Envelopes with Variants

In this grouping, *variant* refers to any word, phrase or line Dickinson preceded with a + mark in the poem corresponding to any word, phrase or line preceded by a + mark annotated at the end or on the margins of the poem. Manuscripts where variant words are stacked closely in proximity, unaccompanied by + marks, have also been included.

A 105

A 105a

A 108

A 109

A 139

A 140

A 145 / 146

A 165

A 193 / 194

A 201

A 202

A 232

A 236

A 252

A 277

A 278

A 316

A 317

A 320

A 332

A 339

A 355

A 364

A 391

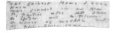

A 394 / 394a

A 438

A 449

A 450

A 464

A 479

A 488

A 496 / 497

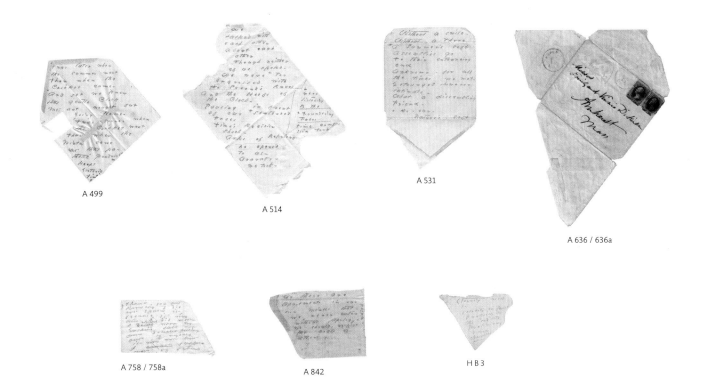

A 499

A 514

A 531

A 636 / 636a

A 758 / 758a

A 842

H B 3

A 193 / 194

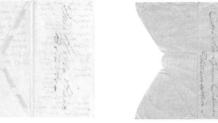

A 165

A 145 / 146

A 140

A 139

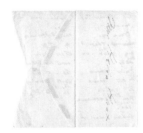

A 317

A 316

A 313 / 314

A 278

A 277

A 394 / 394a

A 391

A 367

A 364

A 355

A 499

A 496 / 497

A 488

A 479

A 464

H B 3

A 865

A 844

A 843

A 842

A 821

A 857

A 139

A 140

A 145 / 146

A 165

A 193 / 194

A 277

A 278

A 313 / 314

A 316

A 317

A 394 / 394a

A 355

A 364

A 367

A 391

A 464

A 479

A 488

A 496 / 497

A 499

A 842

A 843

A 844

A 821

A 857

A 865

H B 3

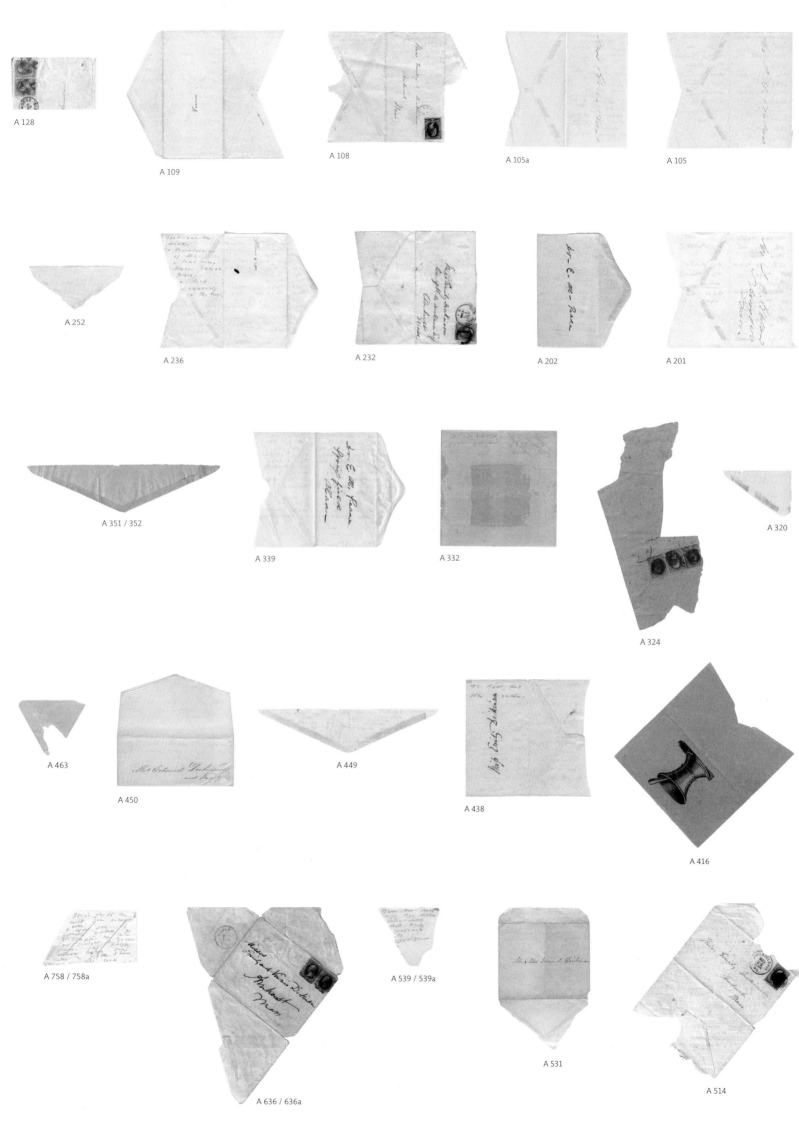

A 128

A 109

A 108

A 105a

A 105

A 252

A 236

A 232

A 202

A 201

A 351 / 352

A 339

A 332

A 320

A 324

A 463

A 450

A 449

A 438

A 416

A 758 / 758a

A 636 / 636a

A 539 / 539a

A 531

A 514

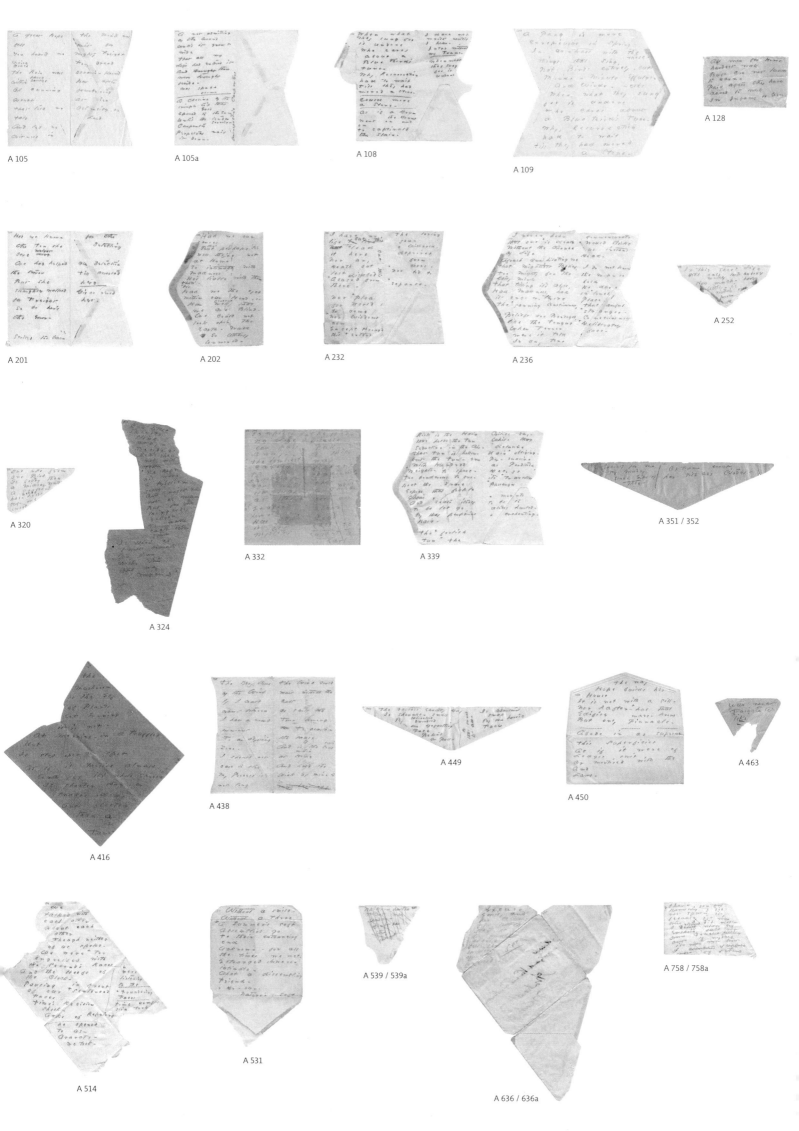

A 105

A 105a

A 108

A 109

A 128

A 201

A 202

A 232

A 236

A 252

A 320

A 324

A 332

A 339

A 351 / 352

A 416

A 438

A 449

A 450

A 463

A 514

A 531

A 539 / 539a

A 636 / 636a

A 758 / 758a

A Directory of the Envelope Writings

Marta Werner

The meticulous notes made by Jay Leyda, Thomas H. Johnson, and Ralph W. Franklin about Dickinson's manuscripts enable the identification of many of the poem drafts, message drafts, and other text fragments composed on envelopes. These scholarly notes, supplemented by a preliminary survey of major archives, are the sources for the present directory. Far from claiming definitiveness, however, this directory serves only as a first point of entry into Dickinson's envelope writings. At present, it identifies fifty-two documents. The total number of envelopes carrying texts—especially message drafts—will continue to rise as more come to light in the collections.

With one exception, the envelope writings included here were drawn from the Amherst College Library, Archives & Special Collections. The numbers on the Emily Dickinson manuscripts in the Amherst College Library were assigned by Jay Leyda, who arranged and described the materials while they were housed at the Folger Library in Washington, D.C. Leyda assigned catalog numbers first to the bound poems (80–95); next to the unbound poems and poem fragments (96–540); and finally to the letters, drafts, and prose fragments (541–1012). The poems were numbered alphabetically by first line, and the letters were numbered alphabetically by correspondent. The arrangement within each correspondence was intended by Leyda to be chronological. It should be noted that Leyda's catalog numbers *generally* refer to texts as opposed to documents; the continuation of a given text on the verso of a document or on subsequent fragments or leaves following the first leaf is identified by the unique catalog number plus a small letter (a, b, c, etc.). In practice, however, this cataloging methodology broke down and texts and documents were conflated (see, for example, A 394 / 394a, A 539 / 539a, A 636 / 636a, A 758 / 758a, where at least some readers and editors believe that Leyda has assigned the same number to discrete texts). In the Directory below, a catalog number is repeated (e.g., A 636 / 636a) when it identifies what may be a discrete text.

The single envelope poem not located in the Amherst College Library but included in the present gathering comes from the Emily Dickinson Collection at the Houghton Library, Harvard University. The cataloging prefix "H B" specifies a poem in this Collection with a special association for Martha Dickinson Bianchi.

The writings carried by the envelopes featured here have been published in various sources; and, in some cases, the publication histories are complex, involving constellations of manuscripts rather than single documents. Notes in this directory identify key twentieth- and twenty-first century scholarly sources for the envelope writings; those interested in more complete transmission and publication histories may consult Jay Leyda's cataloging notes at Amherst College as well as Johnson and Franklin's respective variorum editions and my *Radical Scatters*. Dates, here recorded in brackets, are those assigned by Thomas H. Johnson (THJ) and Ralph W. Franklin (RWF). In some cases, dates are grounded in physical evidence (postmarks, issue date of stamps, etc.); in other cases, dates are based on internal evidence; and in still other instances, they are determined solely by handwriting characteristics. The following editions are cited frequently in the notes:

Letters 1958

Johnson, Thomas H., with Theodora Ward, eds., *The Letters of Emily Dickinson*, 3 vols. Cambridge, MA: The Belknap Press of Harvard University Press, 1958. Citations are to Letter (L) or Prose Fragment (PF) number.

OF 1995

Werner, Marta, ed., *Emily Dickinson's Open Folios: Scenes of Reading, Surfaces of Writing*. Ann Arbor: University of Michigan Press, 1995. Citations are to Amherst College Catalog number.

Poems 1955

Johnson, Thomas H., ed., *The Poems of Emily Dickinson*, 3 vols. Cambridge, MA: The Belknap Press of Harvard University Press, 1955. Citations are to Poem (P) number. The notation "n" (e.g., P1586n) indicates that the envelope poem is cited in Johnson's notes accompanying another version of the work.

Poems 1998

Franklin, Ralph W., ed., *The Poems of Emily Dickinson*, 3 vols. Cambridge, MA: The Belknap Press of Harvard University Press, 1998. Citations are to Poem (P) number.

RS 1999–2010

Werner, Marta, ed., *Radical Scatters: Emily Dickinson's Late Fragments and Related Texts*. Ann Arbor, MI: University of Michigan Press, 1999–2007; Lincoln, NE: Center for Digital Research in the Humanities, 2007–present. Citations are to Amherst College Catalog number.

DIRECTORY

A 105, "A great Hope | fell" c. 1868 [THJ]; c. 1870 [RWF]. Penciled poem draft inscribed across the inside of a slit-open envelope addressed in ink in Emily Dickinson's hand to "Dr J. G. Holland." See *Poems* 1955, P1123; *Poems* 1998, P1187 (A).

A 105a, "A not admitting | of the Wound" c. 1868 [THJ]; c. 1870 [RWF]. Penciled poem draft inscribed on the inside of a slit-open envelope addressed in ink in Emily Dickinson's hand to "Mrs Helen Hunt." See *Poems* 1955, P1123; *Poems* 1998, P1188 (A).

A 108, "When what | they sung for | is undone" c. 1877 [THJ]; c. 1881 [RWF]. Penciled poem draft (partial) of "A Pang is more | conspicuous in Spring" inscribed across the inside of an envelope addressed in ink in Louise Norcross's hand to "Miss Emily E. Dickinson | Amherst | Mass." The envelope bears one 3-cent stamp and is postmarked CONCORD MASS FEB 24. See *Poems* 1955, P1530n; *Poems* 1998, P1545 (A).

A 109, "A Pang is more | Conspicuous in Spring" c. 1881 [THJ; RWF]. Penciled poem draft inscribed on the inside of a cast-off envelope addressed in ink to "Vinnie." See *Poems* 1955, P1530; *Poems* 1998, P1545 (B).

A 128, "All men for Honor | hardest work" c. 1871 [THJ; RWF]. Penciled poem draft inscribed on a remnant of yellow envelope addressed in ink in Frances Norcross's hand to "[Dic]kinson." The envelope bears two 3-cent stamps (1870–71 issue) and is postmarked [MILW]AUKEE WIS OCT 6. See *Poems* 1955, P1193; *Poems* 1998, P1205 (A).

A 139, "As old as Woe –" c. 1870 [THJ]; c. 1872 [RWF]. Penciled poem draft inscribed across the inside of a slit-open envelope addressed in pencil in Emily Dickinson's hand to "Mrs Hunt." See *Poems* 1955, P1168; *Poems* 1998, P1259 (A).

A 140, "As Sleigh Bells | seem ↑ <sound> ↓ in Summer" c. 1864 [THJ; RWF]. Penciled poem draft inscribed across a slit-open envelope addressed in ink in ED's hand to "Miss Eliza M. Coleman – | Care Rev Lyman Coleman | Philadelphia –" See *Poems* 1955, P981; *Poems* 1998, P801 (A).

A 145 / 146. A 145, "It will not harm | her magic pace" c. 1872 [THJ]; c. 1870 [RWF]. Penciled poem draft (partial) of "Because He loves | Her." See *Poems* 1955, P1229n; *Poems* 1998, P1183 (B). / A 146, "We introduce | ourselves +" c. 1872 [THJ]; c. 1870 [RWF]. Penciled poem draft. See *Poems* 1955, P1214; *Poems* 1998, P1184 (A). The poem drafts are inscribed respectively on the left and right halves of the inside of an envelope addressed in ink in Emily Dickinson's hand to "Mrs Helen Hunt – | Bethleem –"

A 165, "Death warrants are | supposed to be" c. 1876 [THJ; RWF]. Penciled poem draft inscribed on the inside of an envelope addressed in ink in Clara Newman Turner's hand to Lavinia Dickinson and postmarked NORWICH CT APR 5. See *Poems* 1955, P1375; *Poems* 1998, P1409 (A).

A 193 / 194. A 193, "Glass was | the Street – " c. 1880 [THJ; RWF]. Penciled poem draft. See *Poems* 1955, P1498; *OF* 1995, n.p., A 193, in facsimile; *Poems* 1998, P1518 (A). / A 194, "It came his | turn to beg –" c. 1880 [THJ; RWF]. Penciled poem draft. See *Poems* 1955, P1500; *OF* 1995, n.p., A 194, in facsimile; *Poems* 1998, P1519 (A). The poem drafts are inscribed over both sides of a torn telegraph blank addressed in ink to "Vinnie Dickenson [*sic*] | Care Judge Lord" and marked "paid" by the sender.

A 201, "Had we known | the Ton ↓ <weight> ↓ <Load > ↑ she | bore" c. 1868 [THJ]; c. 1870 [RWF]. Penciled poem draft inscribed across the inside of a slit-open envelope addressed in ink in Emily Dickinson's hand to "Dr J. G. Holland | Springfield | Mass –" See *Poems* 1955, P1124; *Poems* 1998, P1185 (A).

A 202, "Had we our | senses" c. 1873 [THJ; RWF]. Penciled poem draft inscribed across the inside of a cast-off envelope addressed in ink in Lavinia Dickinson's hand to "Dr – E – M – Pease." See *Poems* 1955, P1284; *Poems* 1998, P1310 (A).

A 232, "I have no | life ~~to live~~ ↑ <but this> ↓" c. 1877 [THJ; RWF]. Penciled poem draft inscribed across the inside of an envelope addressed in ink in Josiah Gilbert Holland's hand to "Miss Emily Dickinson | Care of W. A. Dickinson Esq | Amherst | Mass." The envelope bears a 3-cent stamp and is postmarked NEW YORK NY SEP 13 [1876?] 7 PM. See *Poems* 1955, P1398n; *Poems* 1998, P1432 (A).

A 236, "I never hear | that one + is dead" c. 1874 [THJ; RWF]. Penciled poem draft inscribed on parts of both sides of a slit-open envelope incompletely addressed in ink in Lavinia Dickinson's hand to "Mrs. [*name not legible*]." See *Poems* 1955, P1323; *Poems* 1998, P1325 (A).

A 252, "In this short Life" c. 1873 [THJ; RWF]. Penciled poem draft inscribed on the inside of a torn-away envelope flap. See *Poems* 1955, P1287; *Poems* 1998, P1292 (A).

A 277, "Long Years | apart – can" c. 1876 [THJ; RWF]. Penciled poem draft inscribed on parts of both sides of a slit-open envelope addressed in ink in Abigail I. Cooper's hand to "Miss Vinnie Dickinson." See *Poems* 1955, P1383; *Poems* 1998, P1405 (A).

A 278, "Look back | on Time" c. 1879 [THJ]; c. 1872 [RWF]. Penciled poem draft inscribed on the inside of a torn envelope addressed in pencil in Emily Dickinson's hand to "Little Maggie –" See *Poems* 1955, P1478; *Poems* 1998, P1251 (A).

A 313 / 314. A 313, "Myself compu- | ted were they | Pearls" c. 1874 [THJ]; c. 1873 [RWF]. Penciled poem draft (fragment) of "A Drop fell on the | Apple Tree –" See *Poems* 1955, P794n; *Poems* 1998, P846 (C); *RS* 1999/2010, n.p., A 313, in facsimile. / A 314, "Oh Magnanimity –" c. 1874 [THJ]; c. 1873 [RWF]. Penciled poem draft (fragment) of "'Remember me' | implored the Thief!" See *Poems* 1955, P794n; *Poems* 1998, P1208 (B); *RS* 1999/2010, n.p., A 314, in facsimile. Both poem fragments are inscribed on the inside of an envelope addressed in ink in Emily Dickinson's hand to "Mrs Holland – "

A 316, "Oh Sumptuous | moment" c. 1868 [THJ]; c. 1870 [RWF]. Penciled poem draft inscribed across the inside of a slit-open envelope addressed in ink in Emily Dickinson's hand to "Mrs Helen Hunt." See *Poems* 1955, P1125; *Poems* 1998, P1186 (A).

A 317, "On that | specific Pillow" c. 1881 [THJ; RWF]. Penciled poem draft inscribed on a remnant of paper (A 317) and on a cast-off envelope fragment (A 317a) originally pinned together. The cast-off envelope fragment bears two postmarks: WORCESTER MASS NOV 8 1880 and AMHERST MASS NOV 9 1880. See *Poems* 1955, P1533; *Poems* 1998, P1554 (A).

A 320, "One note from | One Bird" c. last decade [THJ]. Penciled text fragment inscribed on the torn-away flap of an envelope. See *Letters* 1958, PF97; *RS* 1999/2010, n.p., A 320, in facsimile.

A 324, "Our little | secrets | slink | away –" c. 1874 [THJ; RWF]. Penciled poem draft inscribed on a piece of torn brown wrapping paper bearing three stamps (one 3-cent stamp; two 2-cent stamps) and an illegible postmark. See *Poems* 1955, P1326; *Poems* 1998, P1318 (A).

A 332, "Pompless | no Life" c. 1884 [THJ]; c. late 1882 [RWF]. Penciled poem draft inscribed across both sides of a mailing wrapper(?). See *Poems* 1955, P1626n; *Poems* 1998, P1594 (A); *RS* 1999/2010, n.p., A 332, in facsimile.

A 339, "Risk is the Hair | that holds the Tun" c. 1872 [THJ; RWF]. Penciled poem draft inscribed across the inside of a slit-open envelope addressed in ink in Lavinia Dickinson's hand to "Dr. E. M. Pease | Springfield | Mass –" See *Poems* 1955, P1239; *Poems* 1998, 1253 (A); *RS* 1999/2010, n.p., A 339, in facsimile.

A 351 / 352. A 351, "Society for me | my misery" c. 1881 [THJ]; c. 1871 [RWF]. Penciled poem draft. See *Poems* 1955, P1534; *Poems* 1998, P1195 (A); *RS* 1999/2010, n.p., A 351, in facsimile. / A 352, "Or Fame erect | her siteless Citadel –" c. 1881 [THJ]; c. 1871 [RWF]. Penciled poem draft (fragment) of "Step lightly on | this narrow spot –" See *Poems* 1955, P1534n; *Letters* 1958, PF98; *Poems* 1998, P1227 (B); *RS* 1999/2010, n.p., A 352, in facsimile. Both poem drafts are inscribed on the torn-away flap of an envelope.

A 355, "Some Wretched | creature, savior | take" c. 1867 [THJ; RWF]. Penciled poem draft inscribed on a remnant of envelope. See *Poems* 1955, P1111; *Poems* 1998, P1132 (A).

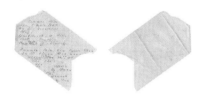

A 364, "Summer laid | her simple Hat" c. October 1876 [THJ; RWF]. Penciled poem draft inscribed across a remnant of envelope addressed in ink in an unidentified hand to "Mr & Mrs Dickinson." See *Poems* 1955, P1363n; *Poems* 1998, P1411 (A).

A 367, "Surprise is like | a thrilling – pungent –" c. 1874 [THJ; RWF]. Penciled poem draft inscribed on the inside of a slit-open envelope addressed in ink in Lavinia Dickinson's hand to "Dr. E. M. Pease." See *Poems* 1955, P1306; *Poems* 1998, P1324 (A).

A 391, "The Ditch | is dear to the | Drunken man" c. 1885 [THJ; RWF]. Penciled poem draft inscribed across the inside of an envelope addressed in ink in ED's hand to "Frank Gilbert – Esq | Hotel Vendome – | Boston – | Mass –" See *Poems* 1955, P1645; *Poems* 1998, P1679 (A).

A 394 / 394a. A 394, "The fairest Home I ever | knew" c. 1877 [THJ; RWF]. Penciled poem draft. See *Poems* 1955, P1423; *Poems* 1998, P1443 (A). / A 394a, "Accept my timid happiness –" c. 1877 [THJ; RWF]. Penciled message draft to Sarah Tuckerman. See *Poems* 1955, P1423n; *Letters* 1958, L528n; *Poems* 1998, P1443n. These fragmentary texts, which may or may not belong to the same composition, are inscribed on both sides of a remnant of envelope addressed in ink in an unknown hand to "Miss Vinnie Dickinson."

A 416, "The | Mushroom | is the Elf | of Plants —" c. 1874 [THJ; RWF]. Penciled poem draft (partial) inscribed across the inside of a slit-open yellow envelope. See *Poems* 1955, P1298n; *Poems* 1998, P1350 (B).

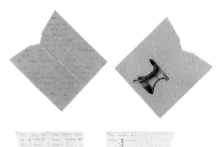

A 438, "The Spry Arms | of the Wind" c. 1866 [THJ]; c. 1864 [RWF]. Penciled poem draft inscribed on both sides of a slit-open envelope addressed in ink in Edward Dickinson's hand to "Miss Emily Dickinson." See *Poems* 1955, P1103; *Poems* 1998, P802 (A).

A 449, "The vastest Earthly Day" c. 1874 [THJ; RWF]. Penciled poem draft inscribed on the torn-away flap of an envelope. See *Poems* 1955, P1328; *Poems* 1998, P1323 (A).

A 450, "The way | Hope builds his | House" c. 1879 [THJ; RWF]. Penciled poem draft inscribed on a cast-off envelope addressed in ink in an unidentified hand to "Mrs Edward Dickinson | and Family." See *Poems* 1955, P1481; *Poems* 1998, P1512 (A).

A 463, "was never | Frigate li" c. 1873 [THJ; RWF]. Penciled poem draft (fragment) of "There is no Frigate | like a Book" inscribed on a remnant of envelope embossed SANFORD & COMPANY, WORCESTER, MASS. See *Poems* 1955, P1263n; *Poems* 1998, P1286 (A); *RS* 1999/2010, n.p., A 463, in facsimile.

A 464, "There's ↑ <That's> ↓ the | Battle of Burgoyne —" c. 1870 [THJ]; c. 1874 [RWF]. Penciled poem draft inscribed across the inside of a slit-open envelope addressed in ink in Frances Norcross's hand to the "Hon. Edward Dickinson | Tremont House | Boston | Mass." The envelope bears the postmark CONCORD MASS. FEB 23; its 3-cent stamp (1873 re-issue) has been canceled. See *Poems* 1955, P1174; *Poems* 1998, P1316 (A).

A 479, "Through what | transports of | Patience" c. 1874 [THJ]; c. 1872 [RWF]. Penciled poem draft inscribed on the inside of a remnant of envelope addressed in ink in Otis Lord's hand to "Miss Emily Dickinson, | Care Hon. Edward Dickinson, | Amherst, | Mass." The envelope bears a 3-cent stamp and the postmark SALEM MASS. NOV 10. See *Poems* 1955, P1153; *OF* 1995, n.p., A 479, in facsimile; *Poems* 1998, P1265 (A).

A 488, "To her | derided Home" c. 1883 [THJ; RWF]. Penciled poem draft inscribed across both sides of a mailing wrapper(?). See *Poems* 1955, P1586n; *Poems* 1998, P1617 (A).

A 496 / 497. A 496, "Tried always | and Condem | ned by thee" c. 1882 [THJ; RWF]. Penciled poem draft. See *Poems* 1955, P1559; *Poems* 1998, P1589 (A). / A 497, "Lives he in any | other world" c. 1882 [THJ; RWF]. Penciled poem draft. See *Poems* 1955, P1557; *Poems* 1998, P1587 (A). These poem drafts are inscribed on both sides of a remnant of a cast-off envelope.

A 499, "'Twas later when | the summer went" c. 1873 [THJ; RWF]. Penciled poem draft inscribed across the inside of a slit-open envelope addressed to "SAMUEL BOWLES, SPRINGFIELD, MASS." by means of a newspaper clipping from the *Springfield Republican*; a stamp, once affixed, was excised before the poem was drafted. See *Poems* 1955, P1276; *Poems* 1998, P1312 (A).

A 514, "We | talked with | each other" c. 1879 [THJ; RWF]. Penciled poem draft inscribed across a slit-open envelope addressed in ink in an unidentified hand to "Miss Emily Dickinson. | Amherst. | Mass." It bears a 3-cent stamp and is postmarked PHILADELPHIA PA. NOV 24 10 AM. See *Poems* 1955, P1473n; *Poems* 1998, P1506 (A); *RS* 1999/2010, n.p., A 514, in facsimile.

A 531, "Without a smile – | Without a Throe" c. 1874 [THJ; RWF]. Penciled poem draft inscribed across the inside of a slit-open envelope addressed in ink in an unidentified hand to "Mr. & Mrs. Edward Dickinson." See *Poems* 1955, P1330; *Poems* 1998, P1340 (A).

A 539 / 539a. A 539, "W̶h̶i̶c̶h̶ ̶–̶ ̶h̶a̶s̶ ̶t̶h̶e̶ ̶|̶ ̶w̶i̶s̶e̶s̶t̶ ̶m̶e̶n̶ ̶|̶ ̶U̶n̶d̶o̶n̶e̶ ̶–̶" c. last decade [THJ]. Penciled text fragment. See *Letters* 1958, PF122; *RS* 1999/2010, n.p., A 539, in facsimile. / 539a, "There are those | who are shallow" c. last decade [THJ]. Penciled text fragment. See *Letters* 1958, PF113; *RS* 1999/2010, n.p., A 539a, in facsimile. Although Johnson separates these text fragments, they almost certainly belong to the same composition inscribed on both sides of a remnant of an envelope flap.

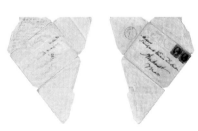

A 636 / 636a. A 636, "Excuse | Emily and | her Atoms" c. October 1882 [THJ; RWF]. Penciled message fragment to Susan Dickinson. See *Letters* 1958, L774n; *RS* 1999/2010, n.p., A 636, in facsimile. / A 636a, "A Mir | acle for | all" c. 1882 [THJ; RWF]. Penciled, fragmentary notes associated with the poem "Pompless | no Life | can pass." See *Letters* 1958, L774n; *Poems* 1998, P1594 (B); *RS* 1999/2010, n.p., A 636a, in facsimile. These text fragments are inscribed on both sides of an envelope addressed in ink in Judge Otis Lord's hand to "Misses | Emily and Vinnie Dickinson | Amherst | Mass." The envelope bears two 3-cent stamps and two postmarks: SALEM MASS DEC 11 and AMHERST MASS DEC [*date illegible*].

A 758 / 758a. A 758, "Thank you for | Knowing I did" c. last decade [THJ].
Penciled message fragment. See *Letters* 1958, PF46; *OF* 1995, n.p., A 758, in
facsimile. / A 758a, "~~It is joy to be | with you because~~" c. last decade [THJ].
Penciled message fragment. See *Letters* 1958, PF40; *OF* 1995, n.p., A 758a, in
facsimile. These message fragments, though separated by Thomas Johnson, may
belong to the same composition and are inscribed on both sides of a remnant
of envelope addressed in ink in an unknown hand to "Miss Dic[kinson]."

A 821, "Clogged | only with | Music, like" c. 1885 [THJ]. Penciled poem
fragment inscribed across the inside of a cast-off envelope (A 821) and over
a separate remnant of an envelope flap (A 821a) originally pinned together.
See *Letters* 1958, L976n; *RS* 1999/2010, n.p., A 821/ A 821a, in facsimile.

A 842, "As there are | Apartments in our" c. last decade [THJ]. Penciled text
fragment inscribed on the inside of a halved envelope addressed in pencil in
Emily Dickinson's hand to "Otis P. Lord | Salem – | Mass –" See *Letters* 1958,
PF21; *OF* 1995, n.p., A 842, in facsimile; *RS* 1999/2010, n.p., A 842, in facsimile.

A 843, "But are not | all Facts Dreams" c. last decade [THJ]. Penciled
text fragment inscribed on a remnant of envelope. See *Letters* 1958, PF22;
OF 1995, n.p., A 843, in facsimile; *RS* 1999/2010, n.p., A 843, in facsimile.

A 844, "But ought not the | Amanuensis ~~also~~ to" c. last decade [THJ].
Penciled text fragment inscribed on a remnant of envelope. See *Letters* 1958,
PF23; *RS* 1999/2010, n.p., A 844, in facsimile.

A 857, "I never saw | Mrs Jackson" c. 1885 [THJ]. Penciled message draft
inscribed across two mailing wrappers(?). See *Letters* 1958, L1015.

A 865, "Not to send | errands by John" c. last decade [THJ]. Penciled text
fragment inscribed on torn corner of envelope, possibly watermarked
FAWN. See *Letters* 1958, PF93; *RS* 1999/2010, n.p., A 865, in facsimile.

H B 3 (Ms Am 118.5 [B3]), "Eternity will | be" c. 1874 [THJ]; c. 1875 [RWF].
Penciled poem draft (fragment) of "Two Lengths | has every Day –" inscribed
on the torn-away flap of an envelope. See *Poems* 1955, P1295; *Poems* 1998,
P1354 (A).

As there are
apartments in our
own minds that —
we never enter
without Apology, — which
we should respect
the seals of
others —

842

Acknowledgments

In 1876, Dickinson wrote to her friend Samuel Bowles, "Of your exquisite Act, there can be no Acknowledgment but the Ignominy that Grace gives" (L465). Still, it is our joy to try to honor the many people whose hard work and artistic vision have made this book.

Our work required us to spend many days in the archives of Dickinson's manuscripts. The vast majority of the manuscripts reproduced here are housed in the Amherst College Library. We extend our sincere gratitude to Mike Kelly, Head of Archives & Special Collections, Frost Library, Amherst College, and to Margaret Dakin, Archives & Special Collections Specialist, Frost Library, Amherst College, for their support of this project. Their wide and deep knowledge of Dickinson's papers is matched by their generous commitment to opening the archives for all to see. We are grateful to Leslie Morris, Curator for Modern Books and Manuscripts at the Houghton Library, Harvard University, for her help in tracking down relevant documents and offering unstinted access to the Houghton's Dickinson collection. We thank all the curators for their grace in granting us permission to share this work.

The images of the manuscripts of Emily Dickinson are reproduced courtesy of Amherst College Library, Archives & Special Collections, and the Houghton Library, Harvard University, and Harvard University Press. The President and Fellows of Harvard College assert the sole ownership of and sole right of literary rights and copyrights therein to the texts of Emily Dickinson. Thankful acknowledgment is made to the Harvard University Press for their permission to publish materials from *The Poems of Emily Dickinson*, Thomas H. Johnson, ed., 1955; *The Poems of Emily Dickinson*, Ralph W. Franklin, ed., 1998; and *The Letters of Emily Dickinson*, Thomas H. Johnson, ed., 1958.

While a few of the manuscript images included here made random appearances in the early editions of Dickinson's writings (see, especially, Martha Dickinson Bianchi's *The Single Hound* [1914] and *Emily Dickinson Face to Face* [1932], Mabel Loomis Todd and Millicent Todd Bingham's *Bolts of Melody* [1945], and Millicent Todd Bingham's *Emily Dickinson: A Revelation* [1954]), it is only in the late twentieth century and early twenty-first century that a larger number of Dickinson's envelope-writings came to light in facsimile. In *Emily Dickinson's Open Folios* (1995), five holographs included in the present gathering (A 193 / 194; A 479; A 758; A 842; and A 843) were previously represented; and in *Radical Scatters: An Electronic Archive of Emily Dickinson's Late Fragments and Related Texts, 1870–1886*, fourteen documents included here (A 313 / 314; A 320; A 332; A 339; A 351 / 352; A 463; A 514; A 539; A 636; A 821; A 842; A 843, A 842, A 865) were previously published. We thank the University of Michigan Press and the Center for Digital Research in the Humanities, University of Nebraska, Lincoln, for their generous permission to publish these images in the present gathering. The introduction to Franklin's three-volume variorum of *The Poems of Emily Dickinson* includes a facsimile of H B 3, the single Houghton Library manuscript in this gathering, and A 416. We are grateful to the Harvard University Press for permission to republish these images in color.

The first incarnation of *The Gorgeous Nothings* was published as an artists' book in an edition of sixty copies by Granary Books in 2012. Publisher Steve Clay's early support of this project and other works make him our first collaborator. Without Granary Books' unique mission and the support of the librarians, curators, and collectors who recognized its importance, this work would have remained only an idea.

Christine Burgin and Barbara Epler of New Directions became our second collaborators, creating *The Gorgeous Nothings* anew in this trade edition. For this transformation, we owe a special debt to Laura Lindgren, whose sensitive, austere page design resonates so closely with Dickinson's late aesthetics, and to Jason Burch for his deft, patient rendering of the new transcription designs. We thank both him and Jessica Elsaesser, whose meticulous preparation of the image files shows Dickinson's manuscripts in their best light; Claudia Markey for fielding research queries; and Helen Graves, our copy editor for New Directions.

The genesis of *The Gorgeous Nothings* has another history. The first part of "Itineraries of Escape" is a "variant" of an essay composed on Emily Dickinson's pinned documents: "The Flights of A 821: De-Archivizing the Proceedings of a Birdsong," published in *Voice, Text, Hypertext: Emerging Practices in Textual Studies*, eds. Raimonda Modiano, Leroy F. Searle, and Peter Shillingsburg (Seattle: The University of Washington Press, 2004). The very last section draws on the archive *Radical Scatters*, published first by the University of Michigan Press in 1999 and a decade later by the Center for Digital Research in the Humanities at the University of Nebraska in 2011, currently under the co-directorship of Katherine L. Walter and Kenneth M. Price. We thank these now more distant but not less important collaborators for their contributions.

Other people accompanied and assisted us in our progress towards a final version of *The Gorgeous Nothings*. We are grateful to the organizers who invited us to present materials from our work-in-progress, including Lee Bricetti, Executive Director of Poets House; Stephen Motika, Program Director of Poets House; Christina Davis, Curator of the Woodberry Poetry Room at Harvard University; Jane H. Wald, Executive Director of the Emily Dickinson Museum; Cindy Dickinson, Director of Interpretation and Programming of the Emily Dickinson Museum; Ryan Haley, Librarian in the Miriam and Ira D. Wallach Division of Art, Prints and Photographs, at the New York Public Library; Barbara Cole, Artistic Director, Just Buffalo Literary Center; and to the many people in attendance at these events who offered thoughtful feedback and criticism. We are also grateful to Donald and Patricia Oresman for the opportunity to exhibit their Dickinson manuscripts at Poets House in 2012, and to curator Claire Gilman for exhibiting Emily Dickinson and Robert Walser manuscripts at The Drawing Center in 2013.

The company and conversation and work of still many others—colleagues, friends, artists, curators—encouraged us to continue and refine our work. In this regard, we would like to thank Charles Bernstein, Elizabeth Willis, Steven Jones, Peter Shillingsburg, Martha Nell Smith, Mona Modiano, Wayne Storey, Robert Waterhouse, Cristian Gurtia, Stephanie Sandler, Jena Osman, Brian Teare, Nancy Kuhl, Cole Swensen, Rachel Bers, Karen Emmerich, Logan Esdale, Jody Gladding, Nancy Eimers, Mary Ruefle, Helen Mirra, Julia Fish, Elizabeth Zuba, and Charlotte Lagarde.

Finally, in the Dickinson archives where we have worked, we have sometimes fancied that an unseen hand guided our own, sifting the documents, holding one or another up to the light. That hand belongs to Susan Howe, whose original discoveries among Dickinson's manuscripts encouraged these further forays. To her, whose felicitous joining of historical inquiry with poetic speculation transformed forever the landscape of Dickinson scholarship, we owe the deepest debt: "Sweet Debt of Life – Each Night to owe – / Insolvent – every Noon" (Fascicle 15, *MB* I, 315).